iv

# CHAPTERS

# PROFILES IN OPTIMISM

THOMAS STOWE MULLIKIN

Vox Populi Publishers, LLC
100 North Tryon Street, Suite 4700
Charlotte, NC 28202-4003

10 9 8 7 6 5 4 3 2 1

ISBN      978-0-9828540-0-6
          978-0-9828540-1-3

Printed in the United States of America.

# PROFILES IN OPTIMISM

THOMAS STOWE MULLIKIN

# INTRODUCTION

I was introduced early to the necessity for unbridled optimism.

It was 1960, the year John F. Kennedy was elected our country's 35th President, that I was born in rural eastern North Carolina. My father was a textile fibers mill worker and World War II veteran; my mother was the daughter of a rural police officer and magistrate. Before I was even a day old, my feet and legs were encased in casts that rose to the hips — the result of a severe case of clubfeet — and my parents were told that it was unlikely I would ever walk. My mother's first glimpse of the second of her fraternal twins was clouded with disbelief and the profound sense that I looked more like a "pretzel" than a baby boy. Throughout most of my early childhood years I was in and out of casts, wheelchairs and walkers. But my parents understood that to survive I needed to work, and to work I needed to overcome my handicap. So they pushed me — sometimes hard, sometimes gently, but never without purpose — and I went on to walk, and run, and climb many mountains.

This book emerged from that climb. Thanks to the love and steady hands of my parents, the opportunities of our great country and the enduring faith of our Lord, I have exceeded my greatest expectations. I want to thank my dedicated team that helped me research, edit and prepare this manuscript. In particular, I appreciate the work of Tania Archer, Kathryn Daniel, Laurie DiGaetano, Meghan Ganio, Joel Groves, Leslie Pedernales, Lindsay Schroeder, Robert Sheppard, Emily Wall and Kira Whitacre.

We live in a day where love of family, country and God can provide the foundation for a lifetime of success and prosperity. My family is extended and includes my wife of 28 years, Virginia Ann, and our four children, Mary Elizabeth, Alexandra, Thomas Jr., and Margaret Charles. But within that extended family, I also include my work family, where I spend many of my waking hours. Nancy Sara, Ski, JR, 6, Wiz, Rock and more than 50 additional members of my "work family" give me the faith and confidence to meet any challenge at work. My "boys" that I grew up with as a "Coach," mentor and friend provide me even greater inspiration; it is through their accomplishments that I find one of the greatest sources of pride. Thank you Vonnie, Eric, Donovan and many other young men in whose eyes I saw determination and optimism.

What is winning when you start ahead? When the team that is undoubtedly going to win does— in fact, win—is it a real and satisfying victory? Or is there greater achievement in a team whose triumph may not necessarily lie in the end game, but in the willingness to "slug it out" on the sometimes arduous, step-by-step path to progress? The fact is, winning is not really the destination. It is the road we walk and the attitude and determination we carry with us along the way. As King David said in Psalm 39, "life is but a mere handbreadth in the face of the Lord; Men go to and fro gathering wealth never knowing where it will go." With life so short, the determination and, yes, optimism that characterize our life's walk will be the mark of our success.

Is the determination of success only the dollars in our checkbook? Or is it really the road we have traveled, the lives we have touched, the mountains we have climbed? I cannot speak for everyone. I can, however, say that while I came into the world with no money and deformed feet, I never lacked for optimism — optimism that life is full of reward for those who seize every opportunity, who help others along the way and who create a lifetime of positive memories with friends that can be shared over and over again. If my life can be measured by these milestones, and not simply by the dollars in my checkbook, the destination will be success.

I have heard it said that 90 percent of life is just showing up. Frankly, I believe this number may be conservative. As a child I remember my profound desire to compete and win in athletics. My family didn't have a great deal of money for camps and equipment, so I had to learn the game on my own and use whatever hand-me-down or cast-off equipment I could find. It was part of the family ethic: Dad did not believe in "giving" a boy too much, feeling that to whom much is given, much goes unappreciated. A young man had to earn his spot in the world.

My father certainly earned his. He spent his formative late-teen years in Germany as part of a special operations reconnaissance unit, providing critical intelligence for the Allied Forces. Among the honors he earned for his efforts were a Bronze Star for Valor and a Purple Heart for being wounded in action. But the awards were secondary to the ultimate lesson of war: learning the value and opportunity of freedom. As was the case with so many others who comprised the "Greatest Generation," this philosophy both drove and directed his life, fostering the optimism that any man or woman could accomplish anything they put their minds to achieving. There was no place in his world for class or race barriers. Life was about the belief in self, and optimism was its foundation. It was through this paradigm that he raised his five children.

My mother was raised in some of the poorest circumstances imaginable. "Poor" takes on a different meaning in eastern North Carolina where there is no safety net and pride prevents many from accepting any kind of hand-out. Paul said in 2 Thessalonians 3:10-11 that "if a man shall not work, he shall not eat." My mother was raised with a clear understanding of this directive.

The parable of David meeting Goliath told in 2 Samuel provides insight into one of the most extraordinary displays of optimism and courage ever chronicled. No man, not even the greatest warrior, was brave enough to meet Goliath. Only David — a shepherd boy armed with a slingshot and a determination that surpassed that of others who were stronger and better equipped — stepped up for the Israelites and volunteered to confront this fearsome enemy. It is safe to say that the odds were heavily stacked against David, but this courageous young man certainly defied them. He accepted the challenge of a lifetime and changed the course of human history.

How often have we seen our friends and family fail to take on a challenge because the odds were against them? How often have we refused to allow ourselves to be tested out of fear — whether it was the fear of getting hurt, of defeat, of losing face or of letting down our families? But in many ways, that is what life is all about: a willingness to accept the challenges — the small ones as well as the great ones — that are a natural part of our day-to-day existence. Better stated, if you want to win, you have to compete.

But so often, the difference between winning and losing is slight, perhaps even imperceptible, and maybe even impossible to calibrate. After all, what separates an A student from a C student may be nothing more than 10 or 15 minutes of extra study each day. It is no different in the workplace. The difference in delivering the best product or performance may well be just a matter of confidence, the determination to go "above and beyond" and a fundamental belief that nothing is impossible.

In other words, optimism.

This book is about that kind of optimism. The people profiled in these pages embraced optimism not for its own sake, or as a crutch, or as a shield to deflect the sometimes harsh realities of their life and times. Rather, they used it to get them through dark times, to hurdle seemingly insurmountable barriers, to fight society's narrow-mindedness, or to pursue a dream. Their optimism was manifested in many ways: personal strength, physical courage, persistence, faith, the quest for fairness, clarity of vision and the fight against outdated and unjust mores. But no matter what the form or intent, it was always genuine, fueled by the belief that good will and the better side of human nature would always prevail.

These are important messages. For our challenges are as great today as they have been since the birth of America. We are losing jobs at alarming rates to foreign countries. Our climate is changing. Our families are working harder and earning less. Our institutions — political, economic and social — are under siege. Life and its obstacles are more complex than ever. We need to rejuvenate ourselves, our communities, our cities and our states so we can face, head-on and through studied consideration and open debate, the difficulties of the day.

But most of all, we need to move forward with the confidence and unaltered optimism that we not only live in the greatest country ever created but also that we can overcome the greatest challenges in life. In 1968, Dr. Martin Luther King Jr. said that while there were "difficult days ahead. . . it doesn't matter with me now. Because I've been to the mountaintop." Similarly, Bobby Kennedy reminded us that "when a man stands for an ideal or acts to improve the lot of others, he sends forth a tiny ripple of hope that when combined with other centers of energy can overcome even the greatest barriers."

We may not be at the mountaintop yet. But we will get there. And we will be propelled to these heights by optimism, the "ripple of hope" that will help us confront the complications and uncertainties that are sure to mark our ascent.

At the signing of the Declaration of Independence, Benjamin Franklin said: "We must all hang together, or assuredly we shall all hang separately." In many ways, this profound statement speaks directly to our present dilemma. While the speed of national and global events may indeed leave our heads spinning, and the nasty partisan debates may leave us thirsting for leadership, we cannot fail to recognize the threshold need to come together first as Americans. It is time for all of us to stand up as citizens of this great land — not as representatives of competing ideologies or political parties or special interests — and to affirm that no matter how bitter the trial or steep the mountain, we can prevail. We need only to be optimistic.

Will that be easy?

No. But achieving what is great and necessary and rewarding rarely is. In the pages that follow, you will read about historic challenges and the unwavering optimism that each of these heroes demonstrate in meeting their burdens.

I hope that those who read this survey and study of determined optimism will simply embrace the message. This world that we live in and this great country that we have formed offers unbounded opportunity for those who are willing to pick up their strengths, their dreams and move forward with unbridled optimism. May we all embrace the challenge of our day and leave the lasting legacy that even the greatest dreams can come true with dedication, determination and optimism!

# RAY CHARLES

When Ray Charles arrived at a school for the blind in St. Augustine, Florida, he was immediately struck by the ludicrousness of the segregated South. Children who could not see were fastidiously segregated by race. Mixing of the races was strictly forbidden. Ray realized at the tender age of seven years old that he would have to overcome the handicap of his skin color as well as the handicap of his blindness. It was a challenge he met with both enthusiasm and optimism.

Ray Charles was born into stark poverty to an unwed young mother in 1930s America. Life was bound to be difficult for any young black man living under Jim Crow laws in the South. While this environment alone presented challenges, for Charles it served as the backdrop against which he would face many struggles, including surviving three devastating life experiences before the age of 15. Any one of these tests could have broken the hope and punctured the optimism of a typical individual. But Ray Charles was anything but typical.

It was during these tests that young Ray turned to the music within. In his autobiography, *Brother Ray*, he says, "I was born with music inside me. . . Music was one of my parts. Like my ribs, my kidneys, my liver, my heart. Like my blood. It was a force already within me when I arrived on the scene."[1]

Song was a constant source of comfort and was present through the good times and the bad. The bad times included his younger brother drowning in a washbasin when Charles was five and his eyesight fading into darkness at seven. But beyond these tragic events, Charles describes his mother's death when he was 15 as the single most devastating moment of his life. It left him alone in a world without sight. Yet within that world—or perhaps despite it—he found optimism.

With the death of his mother, Charles decided to follow his music where it took him. By whole-heartedly living his talent, he absolutely thrived, earning his much-deserved title "The Genius of Soul" along the way. Throughout his career, Charles pushed recording industry boundaries with his genre-bending sound and business savvy. And he

---

[1] Ray Charles and David Ritz. *Brother Ray* (Cambridge, MA: Da Capo Press, 2004), 8.

did it by calling on his unapologetic perseverance and innate survival instincts; by consistently demonstrating the good sense to adapt to whatever curveballs life threw his way; and by never surrendering his optimism to the challenges of the moment.

The greatness of Ray Charles dates back to his youth, and to the Red Wing Café in Greenville, Florida. He had barely learned to walk before seeking out the old stand-up piano and jukebox at the Red Wing. He remembers listening to and learning from Wylie Pitman as he played boogie-woogie. "He saw I was willing to give up my playing time for the piano, so I guess he figured I loved music as much as he did," Charles recalled of that first encounter with the instrument that would eventually help him earn a dozen Grammy Awards. "And all this was happening when I was only three."[2]

A good mama's boy, young Ray could faithfully be found at church, singing along to the hymns that would become so instrumental to his signature sound, which merged gospel and blues. A *New York Times* article announcing his 2004 death captures "The Genius" essence best: "He could conjure exaltation, sorrow and determination within a single phrase."[3] Southern preachers hoped to achieve that every Sunday morning. Ray Charles achieved it every time he sang a note.

His hard-working mother held many jobs, but washing people's clothes was a primary source of family income. Her large washbasin was often a haven where her boys would cool off and play during those unbearably hot Florida summer days. But when Ray was five and his brother George was four, the washbasin became the scene of tragedy. In his autobiography, Charles recounts watching George flailing away in the water, first thinking his brother was playing, but then realizing that he was in serious trouble: "I run—run to the house like I'm on fire, yelling, hollering, crying for Mama who's at the ironing board. She drops everything and comes running, pulls George from the tub and tries to breathe life into him. . . She's drowning in her own tears."[4] George was dead.

---

[2] Charles and Ritz, Ibid, 9.
[3] John Pareles, "Ray Charles, Who Reshaped American Music, Dies at 73." *New York Times*. June 10, 2004.
[4] Charles and Ritz, Ibid, 13.

"It was a powerful thing to have witnessed," Charles said. "And it came at a strange time in my life. Turned out to be one of the last things I would ever see."[5]

Only months after his brother drowned, Charles' eyesight began to slip away, most likely due to an untreated glaucoma condition. "Going blind. Sounds like a fate worse than death, doesn't it?" he asks in his autobiography.[6] "Well, I'm here to tell you that it didn't happen that way—at least not with me." He attributes his uncanny calmness surrounding the experience to the gradual loss of sight, which had begun two years earlier when he was five.

Charles wasn't a "typical" blind person in terms of relying on aids to get by. He didn't count steps, and he certainly never wanted a guide dog or a cane. At once a realist and an optimist, he said, "It wasn't that I wanted to fool myself. Hell, I knew I was blind as a bat. But I didn't want to go limping around like I was half-dead. I didn't want to have to depend upon anyone or anything other than myself."[7] He simply adapted. "That's one way of looking at my life," Charles said. "I was able to adjust."[8]

While hardly a fair comparison, I can empathize with his adjustment. In my early childhood, school children made fun of the way I walked. My surgeries had corrected much of my disability but had left my feet very unbalanced because my heels were much higher than the balls of my feet. My classmates ridiculed the way I bobbed on the balls of my feet.

A small handicap and evidence of greater problems to come, which marks others born with similar deformities, I simply taught myself to walk by never straightening out my legs so my heels would hit before the balls of my feet. A seemingly modest adjustment when compared to others such as Ray with enormous handicaps.

Charles' adaptability was evident to those around him. Valerie Ervin, who served as his executive assistant for 10 years at Ray Charles Enterprises, vouches for his ability to get by. "Being the assistant to Mr. Charles was consistent with being an assistant to a sighted person...

---

[5] Ibid, 13.
[6] Ibid, 15.
[7] Ibid, 41.
[8] Ibid, 21.

There was no difference because of his blindness. He was a business man."[9]

That's not to say his ability to adjust wasn't tested. People took advantage of his handicap in the early years, shorting him cash after a performance, for example, or just generally underestimating him because of his blindness. But Charles quickly proved no one should mistakenly assume they could do so and went on to display groundbreaking independence when it came to managing his music and his career. He simply did not allow his limitations to get in the way of his success. Ray consistently relied on the perseverance and resolve that would define his life and career.

These traits were undoubtedly embedded in him from his mother, whom he described as a staunch disciplinarian. She also planted the seeds of self-sufficiency long before Charles was robbed of his sight. "She let me roam, let me make my own mistakes, let me discover the world for myself," Charles said in his autobiography, remembering his childhood.[10] His mother's lessons also prepared him for survival in a world of poverty and segregation and fostered the kind of optimism that kept him going in good times and bad.

Charles' mother was wise enough to know that he needed an education and that it was outside her ability to provide it. Going away to school was the only way Ray could get the education he needed.

So Ray was put on board a train bound for St. Augustine. He recalled in his autobiography how leaving his mother and sister seemed more than he could bear:

> "Mama," I cried, "don't make me go, Mama. I wanna stay with you," But she remained firm.
> "You gotta go, son. How else you gonna learn to read and write? I can only take you so far."[11]

Later, one of the worst times in young Ray's life that required his optimism to sustain him occurred after the untimely death of his mother. Her death was a tragedy he aptly described in a chapter of his

---

[9] Susan Lacy, "PBS: Ray Charles: The Genius of Soul." Interview with Valerie Ervin. PBS. May 19, 2005.
[10] Charles and Ritz, Ibid, 6.
[11] Ibid, 18.

autobiography he titled "Suffering." She had warned him, in the early days when he was learning life's ropes — "I'm not always going to be with you."[12] But she was young, and he was young, and the concept of death seemed beyond imagination. But when he was 15 and away at school in St. Augustine, Ray got the news of the unimaginable. He hadn't seen his mother for months. There had been no time for goodbyes. "Mama was gone, and now I had to figure out what I was going to do with the rest of my life," Ray remembered of the funeral. "Standing there by the grave, in spite of the folks surrounding me, I had never felt so alone."[13]

A week of despair settled in, threatening Ray's trademark optimism and resilience. Although he knew, deep down, that his mother would not want him wallowing in pity or misery, his grief was as solitary as it was unbearable. But help arrived in the person of Ma Beck, a Greenville neighbor and a mother of 22 children ("Concerning matters of the soul, she knew her business" Charles wrote in his autobiography) who went about administering some tough love. "You gotta carry on," she said. "That's all there is to it. That's what she'd want. And that's what you gotta do. You gotta carry on, RC."[14] That's exactly what Charles did for the next 58 years of his life. But the pain of his mother's passing had left an invisible scar. "That week of silence and suffering also made me harder, and that hardness stayed with me the rest of my life," Charles said.[15]

Back home on summer break, working his way out of despondence, Charles did a lot of "what next" thinking. Eventually, two options surfaced: he could return to St. Augustine and continue in the all-expense-paid school in the fall. Or, he could simply quit.[16] He chose the latter. And before long, the teen was on a train bound for Jacksonville, Florida, more than 100 miles from home, chasing his dream of singing in front of paying crowds.

In many ways, Charles' enormous optimism was a product of his music. It had a unique power to lift him above troubles and tragedy and to guide him through the darkest of hours. The effect was not lost on him. "I could sense something ticking inside me — a rhythm, a beat, a

---

12 Ibid, 58.
13 Ibid, 62.
14 Ibid, 61.
15 Ibid, 62.
16 Ibid, 63.

pulse — something very strong and very steady. Even with all the wild fears and terrible pain brought on by Mama's death, I could feel a new sensation: I was starting to have a little faith. . . in myself."[17]

"From these experiences as much as any springs the empathy that vibrates in Ray Charles' music," writes Michael Lydon, who professionally followed Charles for years as a founding editor at *Rolling Stone*.[18] "The event engraved itself in the young man's heart, to be worked out in song for the rest of his life."

While in Jacksonville, Lydon says, Charles struggled to hold his own. But he never gave up and, as his natural aptitude for music surfaced, obstacles quickly gave way to opportunities:

> He had perfect pitch and could hear the whole combo
> and each instrument's distinct voice at the same time.
> Blindness posed no handicap in learning song forms
> and chord sequences—all musicians visualize the
> structure of music in the darkness of the mind's eye—
> and his aptitude for math gave him an advantage.[19]

In Jacksonville, Charles joined the Local Union 632 as a professional musician and played with his first big band, led by Henry Washington.[20] Between learning the classics at school, from Bach to Chopin, and mimicking the varied sounds on the radio and jukebox, Charles showed an early ability to perform an array of musical styles. "Once I started playing in the big city, I could jump back and forth from different styles— doing boogie here or playing big-band swing there— depending on how the boss wanted."[21]

Although the Jacksonville experience confirmed his talents and reinforced his optimism, the urge to move on was strong. So at age 16 and completely on his own, Charles went to Orlando. The change of scenery initially was not for the better. "These were my hardest days," Charles says in his autobiography, "and sometimes in Orlando I actually wondered whether I was going to starve to death."[22] The music scene

---

[17] Ibid, 65.
[18] Lydon, Michael. *Ray Charles: Man and Music*. (London: Routledge, 2004), 24.
[19] Ibid, 34.
[20] Charles and Ritz, Ibid, 69-70.
[21] Ibid, 72.
[22] Charles and Ritz, Ibid, 75.

there was highly competitive, which made earning a paycheck tough. But Ray Charles knew he could do it. He just needed to adapt. And he did, furthering his career — and his marketability — by turning his blindness into a talent for arranging music. According to Lydon:

> Since RC couldn't scratch out rough drafts of his ideas as most arrangers do, he worked out complete charts in his head, every voice top to bottom, then dictated the parts to the other musician, calling out what he wanted each instrument to play. ... This dictating method, one Charles would use for years, proved RC's uncommon musical ability to all the musicians in town.[23]

But setbacks accompanied success. The national act headed by Lucky Millinder was in town auditioning for piano players. Urged by friends, Charles tried out. He stepped onto the stage with bravado, performed a few selections, then waited for the verdict. Millinder simply said, "Ain't good enough, kid."[24] Charles' hopes were dashed. While the rejection stung and remained with him for years, Charles characteristically located a positive within the disappointment. "What Lucky did to me was make me stop kidding myself," he explained in a 1985 interview. "I learned you aren't good just because people around you say you are good!"[25] The lesson was clear: use the criticism from others to better yourself.

Charles continued to do just that, focusing on a lifelong "quest for quality" in his work. In the 1950s, while the uncertain days of landing gigs were gone, he did not slack off. Hank Crawford, Charles' saxophone sideman, remembers the band having more gigs and larger audiences, but Charles was still a stickler for perfection. "If you couldn't play the music right," said Crawford, "Ray'd fire you, no matter whether we had a replacement — you gotta go."[26] Charles' goal then, as it would be forever, was simply to produce the best possible product.

---

[23] Michael Lyndon, *Ray Charles: Man and Music.* (London: Routledge, 2004), 41.
[24] Ibid, 43.
[25] Ibid, 43.
[26] Lydon, Ibid, 152.

He signed with Atlantic Records in 1952, a year that opened the door for his transformation. While Ray's music contained the sadness of blues, his optimism shone through in the Southern gospel music he infused into the final product. An article posted on the Rock and Roll Hall of Fame's web site about Charles, who was one of the Hall's inaugural inductees, states: "While recording for Atlantic Records during the 1950s, the innovative singer, pianist and bandleader broke down the barriers between sacred and secular music. The gospel sound he'd heard growing up in the church found its way into the music he made as an adult."

The Rock Hall also notes that when "I Got a Woman" hit No. 2 on the R&B charts in March 1955, it was the first song to be labeled as "soul." Hence, "The Genius of Soul" moniker was born.

Another example of Charles' ability to blend church songs that Southern parishioners knew by heart is his reworking of "My Jesus Is All the World to Me" into "Hallelujah, I Love Her So." The most famous and lucrative of these secular crossovers was "What'd I Say," which in 1959 helped Charles achieve his first Gold Record. He took the gospel-secular connection one step further by adding a group of female singers to his act, The "Raelettes," a trio that added a vocal style similar to a black church choir.

The resulting sound became a high-energy celebration of life and love and love lost. Charles' music was the vehicle by which his eternal optimism and expectation of positive outcomes in all areas of his life took flight. The band had become a force in music, propelled in no small part by Charles' continuing success in producing a diverse range of styles. The Grammy Awards of the early 1960s more than took note. He won a pop Grammy for the soulful ballad "Georgia on My Mind" in 1960; captured an R&B Grammy in 1961 for "Hit the Road, Jack;" and landed his third straight in 1962 with a country hit, "I Can't Stop Loving You."

"There will never be another musician who did as much to break down the perceived walls of musical genres," said Ray's longtime friend and recording legend Quincy Jones.[27]

The foray into country says a lot about Charles' gifts and his unyielding belief in himself. As he set out to produce *Modern Sounds in*

---

[27] Chris Heard, "Lasting Influence of legend Charles." *BBC News.* February 14, 2005, news.bbc.co.uk/2/hi/entertainment/3797311.stm.

*Country and Western Music* in 1962, there was some resistance at his record label, which feared its lucrative artist might alienate his fan base with such a drastic change. Charles was willing to take an artistic risk because commercial success was not the primary issue. He believed his own optimistic spirit could add an innovative sound to familiar country standards. Besides, he says in his autobiography, he had his own special appreciation for country tunes because he had been listening to the Grand Ole Opry since childhood.

So the switch to country music should not have been a surprise. "I was only interested in two things: being true to myself and true to the music. I wasn't trying to be the first black country singer. I only wanted to take country songs and sing them my way, not the country way."[28] What emerged was the album that included such hits as "Take These Chains," "You Are My Sunshine" and the Grammy-winning "Hit the Road, Jack."

This period in his life, from the early 1950s to early 1960s, held many highlights, including a 1959 appearance with the legendary Billie Holiday at Carnegie Hall. It also honed his pursuit of perfection. "I'm sure I was born with some natural musical talent," he says in his autobiography, "but I also know that I've always felt the need to perfect my skills. I still feel the need today. I'll always feel the need because perfection isn't attainable."[29]

Regardless of the question — whether it was the singular focus on getting better or his ability to jump genres — Charles always followed his instincts. Confident of himself and his product, he never stooped to cheap gimmickry to publicize or promote his work, and marketing was always an after-the-fact consideration. "It's not that I'm against marketing," he says in his autobiography. "It's a business, ain't it? But that's after the artist has already made the product itself. After all, the product is me, and I don't see myself as a gimmick."[30] And Ray Charles had supreme faith in that particular product, and an unyielding optimism that he could — and would — overcome whatever barriers life placed in his way.

Blindness, of course, was chief among those obstacles. But Ray Charles was also a black man and a black musician in a segregated

---

[28] Charles and Ritz, Ibid, 223.
[29] Ibid, 68.
[30] Charles and Ritz, Ibid, 226.

America. In his autobiography, Charles remembers one of the earliest impressions of segregation upon arriving at the Florida State School for the Deaf and the Blind in St. Augustine. First, students were separated by skin color, living and learning in separate quarters. They were further segregated into blind groups and deaf groups, then into boys and girls. "Going blind made me even less conscious of it (race)," Charles recalled. "But imagine the nonsense of segregating blind kids. I mean, they can't even see!"[31]

Later in 1960s America, the racial tension was palpable. While Charles could not escape it, he admittedly did not take as active a political stance against segregation as others had during that time. He did, however, refuse to perform in segregated venues, and it cost him. After his first refusal, in Augusta, Georgia, in 1961, he was banned from performing in his home state of Georgia for almost two decades. "Mr. Charles. . . didn't understand any of that because he judged people by who they were, not color," said Valerie Ervin of her former employer. He stood his ground on not performing because the audience was segregated."[32] In addition to refusing segregated venues, Charles also recorded *A Message from the People* in 1972, an album most notable as his first attempt at political commentary by way of song. The final track on the album is the artist's famous and moving rendition of "America the Beautiful."

Charles also performed concerts in support of Dr. Martin Luther King Jr.'s cause. In the chapter of his autobiography titled, "Following a Leader," he explained he wasn't suited to marching for a cause — not because he couldn't see, but due to his somewhat volatile temperament. If personally confronted by violence, Charles conceded he wouldn't be able to hold back from retaliation, and nonviolence was a pillar of King's movement. Always demonstrating a good-natured candor about his blindness, Charles added, "I wouldn't have known when to duck when they started throwing broken beer bottles at my head."[33] He added, more seriously:

31 Ibid, 22.
32 Susan Lacy. "PBS: Ray Charles: The Genius of Soul." Interview with Valerie Ervin. PBS. May 19, 2005.
33 Charles and Ritz, Ibid, 273.

But when the smoke settled and the fires burned themselves out, I could see that of all the people running around, one cat had the clearest and the furthest vision. That was the good Doctor King. They could gun him down and kill him, but they couldn't make us forget his lessons. He taught us, we listened, and now we know.[34]

Then in 1979, after all the racial turmoil, Charles' blend of personal optimism, professional discipline, and pursuit of artistic perfection was formally recognized when the Georgia General Assembly officially welcomed him home. "My version of 'Georgia' became the state song of Georgia. That was a big thing for me, man. It really touched me. Here is a state that used to lynch people like me suddenly declaring my version of a song as its state song. That is touching."[35] Charles said the commemorative performance of the song at the state legislature was a highlight of his life.

What is especially impressive about Ray Charles is that he maintained his positive outlook despite the presence of demons that might have crippled — even killed — a lesser person. To his credit, he never denied them, openly discussing a 17-year heroin addiction and talking about his "enjoyment" of women when performing on the road. He was no hypocrite, either, never preaching about his own perfection or imposing life lessons on others. "I'm not making recommendations, and I don't want anyone to follow my lead, but if I'm going to describe my life accurately, I got to tell you how my drug habit affected me," he recounts candidly in his autobiography. "I don't think it really held me back."

Although Charles claimed the drugs didn't interfere with his music ("One important thing about me and dope: I never lost myself, even just after I shot up. ... I made my gigs, I sang my songs."[36]), they did seriously damage his relationship with second wife Della Beatrice Howard Robinson, or "B." Charles admits, "I regretted that most, but

---

34 Ibid, 276.
35 Jessica McElrath, "Ray Charles Quotes." About.com, July 7, 2009, afroamhistory.about.com/od/raycharles/a/rcharlesquotes.htm, accessed April 14, 2010.
36 Ibid, 181.

not enough to make me quit."[37] Despite everything, though, she was there for the long haul. In Los Angeles she built a home for their three sons: Ray Charles, Jr., David and Robert. Charles' life was playing gigs on the road, but he says in the brief times he spent with family, he respected the home B had built them. She preferred to raise their boys herself, turning down an offer to join Charles on the road as a back-up singer.[38]

A true turning point in Charles' life came in 1964 when federal agents at Boston's Logan Airport caught him with marijuana and heroin. Facing criminal charges, his life, career, and family were suddenly in jeopardy. But Ray Charles employed the same personal strength and courage that had helped him overcome blindness and racism. He immediately checked himself into rehab, determined to get clean. He ignored doctors' suggestions for a slow withdrawal from the powerful grip of addictive substances, instead opting for a cold-turkey approach. He believed it would work. It did. After a year of legal proceedings, he was sentenced to five years of probation. He says he never touched heroin again for fear of losing his family.

In the end, the story of Ray Charles' life is the story of how hope, determination, steadfast perseverance, resolve and, ultimately, optimism changed the way the world grew to appreciate a black, blind man in America. Over his five-decade-long career, Charles received 12 Grammy Awards and a Grammy Lifetime Achievement Award; additionally, he was inducted into the Songwriters Hall of Fame and the Rock and Roll Hall of Fame. Eventually, 60 albums would bear the soulful singer's name — impressive by any standard. But more than that, he showed the world, and himself, the connection between self-belief and personal triumph. Quincy Jones reinforced this in an interview shortly after Charles' death from liver disease in 2004. When Jones was asked, "Is there a quintessential Ray Charles sound?" he replied, "Absolutely. It is the pain converted into joy. It's the darkness converted into light."[39]

[37] Charles and Ritz, Ibid, 185.
[38] Ibid, 186.
[39] Rebecca Leung, "The Genius of Ray Charles," *CBS News: 60 Minutes.* December 26, 2004.
www.cbsnews.com/stories/2004/10/14/60minutes/main649346.shtml, accessed April 14, 2010.

The ups and downs of producing Charles' body of work were captured in the Academy Award-winning film *Ray*, starring Jamie Foxx, released shortly after the singer's death. His long-time assistant Valerie Ervin has said of the film, "Mr. Charles wanted this movie to be an inspiration and a learning experience for all of those people in the world who thought or think that they cannot be somebody."[40]

And that is, indeed, Charles' message. Even if you start life "on the bottom of the ladder looking up at everyone else" as he did, you can climb that ladder — one rung at a time, one day at a time — and make something of your life.[41] Although Charles could not physically see, there's no doubt he always had that top rung in sight. And what drove him ever higher was a fundamental sense that he could go as high and as far as he wanted. For Ray Charles, that was quintessential optimism.

---

[40] Lacy, "PBS: Ray Charles: The Genius of Soul,"Ibid.
[41] Charles and Ritz, Ibid, 4.

# GANDHI

In May 1893, Mohandas Gandhi, a 23-year-old lawyer, decked out in very British striped trousers, a frock coat, patent leather shoes and a turban on his head, boarded a train for Pretoria (South Africa) to represent a client in a lawsuit.[42]

About 9 p.m., when the train reached Maritzburg, the capital of Natal, a white passenger entered the car. Seeing Gandhi, he complained to the railroad officials that a non-white passenger was in first-class. Officials told Gandhi to move to a third-class van compartment reserved for non-whites. Gandhi showed officials his first-class ticket and refused to move, but the railroad employees didn't care. A constable physically led him off the train and removed his luggage. Gandhi, who had left his overcoat on the train, was too embarrassed to ask for it. He sat shivering in the station as the train pulled away in the night, pondering the significance of what had just happened.[43]

Such an event probably occurred hundreds of times a day in the apartheid culture of South Africa. And this incident, which was peaceful, may not have left an impression on anyone who witnessed it except Gandhi. Yet it would change the history of the world and the destiny of India. The first ugly example of racial prejudice Gandhi had personally experienced, it spurred him to action. According to his biography, he reportedly told an American missionary that the Maritzburg incident was one of the most "creative experiences" of his life. "My active non-violence began from that date."[44]

If there was ever a case to be made for the power of optimism, Gandhi would be a prime example. He took on the world's greatest empire and won, a quest requiring more audacity than even the strongest, most tenacious fighter could muster. The connection between his leadership and his optimism was not lost on historians, one of whom wrote:

---

[42] Sankar Ghose, *Mahatma Gandhi*, (Bombay,[Mumbai]: Allied Publishers Ltd., 1991), 29.
[43] Ibid, 30.
[44] Ibid.

Great leaders need to be great optimists. Optimism about human nature was the starting post of all Gandhi's activities; it sometimes made him sound naive. His optimism sprang from a belief that "man can change his temperament, can control it" although he "cannot eradicate it. God has given him no such liberty." Change and control, therefore, require constant effort.[45]

Gandhi acknowledged the optimism-activism link, saying, "Keep your thoughts positive, because your thoughts become your words. Keep your words positive, because your words become your behaviours. Keep your behaviours positive, because your behaviours become your habits. Keep your habits positive, because your habits become your values. Keep your values positive, because your values become your destiny." The implication is clear: By keeping a strictly positive outlook, the diligent individual can create a snowball effect for good.

The journey of Mohandas K. Gandhi is revered for the propagation of non-violence in opposition to a dying British Empire, leading to the liberated State of India. His quest for Indian independence spanned five decades of racial discrimination, violence and imprisonment on behalf of oppressed populations. His life's work is summed up by the *Satyagraha* paradigm, a philosophy of nonviolent civil disobedience, that was the most powerful resistance to tyranny.

From his early days as a community activist in South Africa through the declaration of the State of India, Gandhi's strength and optimism in the face of adversity were drawn from philosophies on human existence and the power of *swaraj*, which is described as self-rule. He was able to overcome British imperial domination through sacrifice, discipline, faith and a moral devotion to truth. Almost his entire adult life was dedicated to writing, teaching and organizing underserved segments of society around these principles. And although Gandhi's actions were not without critics, his character was tested time and again, ultimately revealing a man of pure intention and heart.

Gandhi began life in a rural community of western India within the princely state of Porbandar. He was the fourth and youngest child of

[45] Louis Fischer, *The Life of Mahatma Gandhi* (New York: Harper & Row, 1950), 81.

Karamchand and Putlibai Gandhi, born Oct. 2, 1869.[46] Very little of his early years is known, but it is clear the young boy enjoyed a comfortable existence due to family lineage. The Gandhi clan traditionally belonged to the Hindu Vaisya caste, a segment of society that functioned not only as merchants throughout history but also operated as *diwans* — or prime ministers — for the ruling authority.[47] As the family held a special place in the local political scene, young Gandhi was privy to a segment of society not common for most Indian children. This exposed him to the influences of elder household members and their acquaintances, which likely began to shape the content of his character.

As Gandhi frequently noted, his parents left an indelible impression on the youngest of their children and played an essential role in whom and what he would become. Karamchand was particularly tenacious. He lacked formal education, but he still was able to thrive in the political confines of his homeland through experience in practical matters.[48] He also had a reputation for opposing corruption and remaining fair-minded in stately activities during a notoriously corrupt period in Indian affairs.

Governing authority over India during the 19th century had largely been enforced through the British East India Company. However, the indigenous population grew wary of the company's growing power, eventually leading to the Great Mutiny of 1857. The British Parliament subsequently consolidated authority under the queen through the Act for the Better Governance of India, and with 550 local princely states dispersed among British-governed territories, the new political structure led to a divide-and-rule policy.[49] It was during this time that Karamchand served with ruling Indian families that were perpetually opulent and corrupt. As historian Yogesh Chadha pointed out, the British allowed discretionary sovereignty within the princely domains, and few rulers allocated funds for the benefit of their citizens.[50] Karamchand served the less-than-noble princely rulers in several capacities, yet always remained loyal to their states.

---

[46] Yogesh Chadha, *Gandhi: A Life*, (New York: John Wiley & Sons, Inc., 1997), 1.
[47] Mahatma Gandhi and Louis Fischer, *The Essential Gandhi: An Anthology of His Writings on His Life, Work and Ideas*, (New York: Vintage Books, a division of Random House, 1962), 4.
[48] Mahatma Gandhi and Mahadev Desai, *Gandhi An Autobiography: The Story of My Experiments with Truth.*, (Boston: Beacon Press, 1962), 4.
[49] Chadha, Ibid, 2.
[50] Ibid.

Although Karamchand's position did not allow for legitimate political authority, it did permit the family to retain a place in middle-class society. Eventually Mohandas would voluntarily disconnect himself from this established network of patronage to struggle on behalf of exploited populations. Contemporary scholars have best explained his obsession with suffering as a tool he used to ignite passion and incite action among the millions of impoverished Indians.[51]

Gandhi's mother Putlibai led a pious existence within the traditions of Jainism, so entirely devoted to prayer and fasting that Gandhi regularly referred to her as being saintly.[52] With roughly 10- to 12-million followers worldwide, Jainism is one of the smallest of the world's major religions, but it has traditions that span the dawn of civilization.[53] Followers believe all living creatures have a soul with the potential to be liberated through transcendence; therefore, all of nature's spiritual creatures should be treated with respect and love. As the political philosophy expert Dennis Dalton notes, the everlasting customs of Gandhi's religious mother would become the driving force behind many of his later convictions.[54] Specifically, Gandhi's tolerance and acceptance of all faiths and people helped him bridge the gap when negotiating for Indian rights and independence. Most importantly, however, these early teachings instilled in him the idea that morality is the basis of righteousness, and truth is the basis of morality. This concept of truth would play an increasingly important role in his life and eventually would become one of the pillars of Gandhi's political model.

Moving through high school and into college, Gandhi seemed to lack any discernible desire to excel in academics. Historians have widely noted his average capabilities as a student and his general self-deprecating tendency in all things scholastic.[55] Upon graduation from high school in Rajkot, he was encouraged by many in his family to take the matriculation exam for law school. Gandhi reluctantly did so,

---

[51] Stanley Wolpert, *Gandhi's Passions: The Life and Legacy of Mahatma Gandhi*, (New York: Oxford University Press, 2001), 4.

[52] Gandhi and Desai, Ibid, 4.

[53] Helmuth Van Glasenapp, *Jainism: An Indian Religion of Salvation*, (New Delhi: Shri Jainendra Press, 1999), 2.

[54] Dennis Dalton, *Mahatma Gandhi: Nonviolent Power into Action*, (New York: Columbia University Press, 1993), 15.

[55] Victoria Sherrow, *Mohandas Gandhi: The Power of the Spirit*, (Minneapolis: Lerner Books, 1994), 28.

narrowly passing the exam and going off to London for his legal education.

The London years do not seem to be a particularly pivotal period in the development of Gandhi's ideology. But they did allow a newly independent young man to experience English cultural norms firsthand, and early examples of his steadfastness in dealing with adverse situations emerged. Prior to his departure, Gandhi's mother was suspicious and determined to keep her youngest son away from the "carnivorous and depraved" customs of the West. She enlisted the help of a Jain monk to administer three solemn vows to her son to ensure he would avoid wine, women and meat.[56] Although the cold and foreign land caused many traditional Indian men to break their religious principles, Gandhi was a man of discipline even during times of weakness. He maintained his abstinence for consuming meat, which also enabled him to gain his first experience as an organizer and leader among London's vegetarian societies.

By the end of his barrister school years, Gandhi had grown to appreciate the world outside of his homeland, and his ambitions began to flourish. He briefly returned to India, but Gandhi was soon summoned to South Africa to assist a prominent trading organization, Dada Abdullah & Company, with a merchant case. He set sail for Africa in April 1893,[57] embarking on an adventure that would awaken his senses to the deep-seated racial prejudice and oppression many Indians were subjected to daily. It was there, in South Africa, that the acclaimed Mahatma's truth began to take shape.

Upon arrival in Natal on the southeastern coast, Gandhi was received by Dada Abdullah, a wealthy merchant and his new employer, and immediately sent to Pretoria to be briefed on the pending case. The trip required travel by train, and Abdullah provided first-class tickets for each leg. The incident that followed is considered a turning point in Gandhi's young life.[58]

As briefly noted earlier, Gandhi's life changing event occurred when he was expelled from the "white only" compartment he had occupied at the Maritzburg train station. Gandhi was then ordered by officers into

---

[56] Chadha, Ibid, 20.
[57] Wolpert, Ibid, 33.
[58] Louis Fischer, *Gandhi: His Life and Message for the World*, (Mentor Books, 1982), 21.

the third-class cabin, traditionally reserved for those of color. He adamantly protested, producing his first-class ticket. The official countered, "That does not matter, you must go to the van compartment, or else. . . a police constable shall push you out."[59] For a young man raised in privilege, the blow to his ego was significant. He departed the train without his luggage, spending the cold night alone on a station bench, deep in thought, and vowing that he would suffer whatever hardships were necessary to eradicate the superficial "disease" and help the livelihood of his fellow Indians.[60] Although he could have simply accepted the circumstances as they were and returned to his life of favor and advantage, Gandhi chose instead to sacrifice his societal position to become a community activist. He would spend the remainder of his life voluntarily sacrificing for the singular purpose of self-rule — *swaraj*.

Following the 1893 incident, Gandhi invested much of his time entrenched in the Abdullah case that had brought him to Africa. But he also continued speaking to the Indian community on issues of law. Of specific importance to him were the so-called "disability laws" that, as Indian scholar Vet Mehta explained, prohibited Indians from owning land or being in the street after 9 p.m. and levied an annual head tax of three pounds.[61]

The disability laws alone served to hinder development of any free and expressive Indian society, but the Natal Assembly attempted to go even further with the introduction of the Franchise Amendment Bill in 1894. Upon passage, the law was intended to deny voting rights to anyone of Indian, Asiatic or Polynesian descent, thereby stunting any possibility of Indian representation in colonial government.[62] This disenfranchisement signaled the need for more organized efforts, and Gandhi began writing extensively on the issue of race in South African society.

His treatise, *Grievances of the British Indians in South Africa,* became known as the Green Pamphlet due to the color of its binding. Historians have noted that it is one of the earliest works of *satyagrahi*

---

59 Chadha, Ibid, 53.
60 Ibid.
61 Ved Mehta, *Mahatma Gandhi and his Apostles,* (New York: The Viking Press, 1977), 101.
62 Marilyn Lake and Henry Reynolds, *Drawing the Global Colour Line: White Men's Countries and the International Challenge of Racial Equality,* (Cambridge: Cambridge University Press, 2008), 119.

principles in which Gandhi recommends conquering hatred with love.[63] Essentially a summary of his previous writings detailing the conditions of Indians in South Africa, it was published when Gandhi returned to India in 1896. Although stories of verbal abuse were widely known and accepted to be true across the African colony, the pamphlet's breakout popularity garnered international media attention and led to a furor among the white Natalian population. Gandhi was quickly becoming a despised figure in South Africa. The tensions would come to a turbulent conclusion upon his return to the port city of Durban.

On December 18, 1897, the SS Courland and two other vessels arrived in Durban carrying roughly 600 Indian immigrants in addition to Gandhi and his family.[64] Local Caucasian communities were skeptical of Gandhi's motives, even accusing him of engaging in intentional mass immigration to further his cause. Subsequently, the Natali port authorities quarantined the ships for 27 days after arrival, citing recent plague outbreaks in India as the cause. Gandhi, however, suspected political motives were behind the decision.

Local authorities were eventually forced to release the tired and distraught passengers. Gandhi made no attempt to disguise his identity from the massive crowds that gathered in Durban as he exited the boat. As historian Arthur Herman describes the scene, an angry white mob descended upon Gandhi, snatching his turban and throwing stones and bricks.[65] Two policemen intervened and brought Gandhi to a local house, but the crowd gathered once again and threatened to lynch the soft-spoken freedom fighter. Fortunately, Gandhi was able to escape and seek refuge in the local police station for two days to avoid the rage of the mob.

Gandhi refused to press charges against his assailants in the days and weeks that followed, a decision that won praise from the community and the press and solidified his image as a noble crusader. He would use this tactic repeatedly throughout the resistance struggle, boldly accepting the consequences of his role — sometimes violence, sometimes legal action — then focus his energy upon gaining widespread public support. Many onlookers found it difficult to

---

63 Chadha, Ibid, 72.
64 Ibid, 75.
65 Arthur Herman, *Gandhi & Churchill: An Epic Rivalry That Destroyed an Empire and Forged our Age*, (New York: Bantam Books, a division of Random House, 2008), 112.

condemn his actions, as Gandhi did not seek revenge for the ill treatment the Indian community faced. He only wished to expose its existence and sought equality based on principles Europeans claimed to represent.

Until this point, Gandhi was largely working within the context of the English Empire. He sought individual freedom and respect, but Gandhi had not called for an end to political institutions and norms that accompanied English rule. If fact, since his early days in London, he had admired and respected the system, behaving like a model citizen and instructing the Indian community to assimilate if they wanted to be treated equally.[66] As the struggle continued, however, he came to understand the inherent hypocrisy of a dominant power exploiting people and land for capitalistic gains. His thinking shifted and, as his worldview changed, his political philosophy fully crystallized into the form of *Satyagraha*.

Never a man attached to money or possessions, Gandhi began to insist that his family return to traditional Indian customs; he even asked that they refuse gifts that were often bestowed upon them. Biographer Yogesh Chadha explains that for the first time, Gandhi truly believed non-possession and service to community were synonymous and used all he gained financially to increase efforts for the struggle.[67] In light of his expanded approach, Gandhi was able to successfully organize a homogenous Indian community during the watershed event of Indian South African tensions.

The Asiatic Registration Ordinance, which became known as the Black Act among Indian populations, was proposed by the Transvaal Government in August 1906 and served as the catalyst for a unified resistance to imperial dominance. It required all Indians, Arabs and Turks to register with the government and carry a certificate, which they had to produce upon official request; failure to do so would lead to a fine of 100 pounds or imprisonment of three months.[68]

Historians report that Gandhi, along with most individuals falling under the law, found the act to be discriminatory and humiliating. The measure did, however, present an opportunity to consolidate opposition

---

[66] Michael J. Nojeim, *Gandhi and King: The Power of Non-Violent Resistance*, (Westport, Connecticut: Greenwood Publishing Group, 2004), 127.
[67] Chadha, Ibid, 121.
[68] Dennis Dalton, Ibid, 13.

efforts into a decisive force. Gandhi called upon his local network to move forward with what he had conceived as an "oath before God," a moral mechanism he often used to enforce strict adherence to the cause. He warned followers, "If having taken such an oath we violate our pledge, we are guilty before God and man."[69] It was a defining moment for opposition efforts and the development of Gandhi's ideology.

Observers have described the initial years of the movement as passive resistance, but the ambiguous connotation and generally submissive tone was not acceptable to the determined leader. In his autobiography, Gandhi notes the deliberate intention of using a native Indian language to describe what he believed to be a truly Indian movement. So although the principles applied to all people in his eyes, he simultaneously understood the significance of unifying the community through cultural branding.

*Satyagraha* came to be the verbal characterization of the Indian struggle. It was created by Gandhi through the combination of two Sanskrit words, *satya* and *agraha*, literally translated as truth and firmness, respectively. He defined the term as "the vindication of truth not by infliction of suffering upon the opponent but on one's self."[70] Scholars have stated that the *Satyagraha* paradigm is Gandhi's most influential contribution to political and civil thought.

As the first *Satyagraha* campaign unfolded in the spring and summer of 1907, the British Indian Association sponsored marches, pickets and speeches, all of which Gandhi was heavily involved. The pressure applied to the government was successful in that the original registration deadline of July 31, 1907, was moved back to October 31 and then to November 30.[71] Romain Rolland, a French humanist and pacifist who wrote about Gandhi, points out that, for the first time, all Asiatic races were bound together in a concerted opposition effort.[72]

To keep the community informed on the state of resistance efforts, Gandhi published articles in his weekly magazine, the *Indian Opinion*. It was during this time that he found strength in Christianity; Gandhi was

[69] M.K. Gandhi, *The Collected Works of Mahatma Gandhi*, (Austin: Greenleaf Books, 1983), Vol. 5, 419-420.
[70] Fischer, *Gandhi: His Life and Message for the World*. Louis, pg. 35.
[71] Herman, Ibid, 155.
[72] Romain Rolland, *Mahatma Gandhi: The Man Who Became One with the Universal Being*, New Delhi: Publications Division, Ministry of Information and Broadcasting, Government of India, 1968), 20.

drawn to the analogy among Christ and the Transvaal Indians, writing more profoundly than he had in the past:

> Gentle Jesus the greatest passive resister the world has seen, is their pattern... Was not Jesus rejected and yet did He not resist the blasphemy that His persecutors would have Him utter on pain of suffering what was, in their estimation, an inglorious death... He dies indeed, yet He lives in the memory of all true sons of God.[73]

Gandhi's writings remained vigilant, yet optimistic that the government would be forced to concede in the face of humiliation generated by the non-violent masses. By the fall of 1907, however, it appeared his initial assumptions were wrong when the Transvaal government began arresting and prosecuting people for their refusal to register. It was only a matter of time before Gandhi would join the burgeoning prison population for failure to obey.

He was arrested and found guilty of the crime of "no registration certificate" in December 1907 and was ordered to leave the colony.[74] Gandhi would no more listen to the authority of the courts than he would recognize the authority of discriminatory laws. So in January 1908, he was again called into court, found in contempt and sentenced to two months in prison alongside several other opposition activists. The sentence would be the first of three for the freedom fighter in South Africa, but as with many things in life, he found great meaning and learned constructive lessons from each prison term. Journalist and Gandhi biographer Louis Fischer noted Gandhi's desire to perform hard labor and undergo sufferings in the interest of his country and religion and wrote that Gandhi found solace in the freedom that prison provided.[75]

Indian struggles continued in a manner consistent with Gandhi's own experience over the next five years. Some individuals were jailed in excess of eight times, and at one point, over 19 percent of the entire

---

73 Gandhi, *The Collected Works,* Vol. 7, 119.
74 Wolpert, Ibid, 66.
75 Fischer, *Gandhi: His Life and Message,* Ibid, 38.

Indian Transvaler population was imprisoned.[76] During this period the South African Minister of Finance and Defense, General Jan Christiaan Smuts, worked tirelessly to enforce the status quo of intolerance and prejudice. He engaged in xenophobic rhetoric and introduced invasive legislation, such as the Asiatic Immigration Bill of 1912, aimed at restricting freedoms and excessively taxing the Indian indentured laborers.[77] Simultaneously, the Cape Colony Supreme Court ruled that only Christian marriages would be legally recognized, much to the shock of Hindus and Muslims alike.

These factors revitalized mass protests and led to what became known as the "Great March." During this march — which by Gandhi's own account included 2,037 men, 127 women and 57 children[78] — several laborers were needlessly shot and killed by white soldiers who claimed to have fired in defense. A public backlash followed, and the ruling authorities were eventually forced to realize that no amount of racial encroachment would be accepted by the Indians. It was only after years of communal sacrifice and discipline on the part of the united community that the South African government began negotiations to mitigate the Indians' long list of grievances.

Scholars describe the agreement between Smuts and Gandhi as a series of discussions from which the language of the Indian Relief Bill was drawn. All major points of contention were addressed, including the recognition of non-Christian marriages and the repeal of certain prohibitive sections of the Asiatic Registration Act, and the bill was adopted by Parliament in the summer of 1914.[79] Smuts conceded after the fact that he was grateful for the opportunity to work with Gandhi during negotiations, stating "his ethical and intellectual attitude, based as it appears to be on a curious compound of mysticism and astuteness, baffles the ordinary process of thought."[80] Through an unyielding devotion to optimism, the goal Gandhi had set for himself at Maritzburg Station some 21 years prior had finally been achieved.

Historians have viewed South Africa as the laboratory for Gandhi's developing ideology. Dennis Dalton, a Gandhi authority, goes so far as to say that what South Africa did to Gandhi was much more significant

---

[76] Ibid, 41.
[77] Wolpert, Ibid, 78.
[78] Gandhi, *The Collected Works*, Vol. 29, 240.
[79] Fischer, Gandhi: His Life and Message, 47.
[80] Wolpert, Ibid, 80.

than what Gandhi did to it.[81] Gandhi arrived on the African continent dressed in traditional European garb, without a voice or a purpose. He faced the adversity at Maritzburg Station, setting in motion a transformational journey that continued on through the Great March and ended with the Indian Relief Bill. As author J.J. Holmes expounds, "At the very opening of his career, this young and inexperienced lawyer, without influence, money or any wide acquaintanceship, was to reveal the courage, resolution, and shrewd resourcefulness which were to characterize his years of patient leadership."[82] The South Africa experiment expanded Gandhi's strength and refined his purpose, and with the help of a willing population, he was able to develop a successful campaign for social and political change.

While the South African government adopted sweeping reforms, Gandhi turned his attention to his homeland where, as his grandson and biographer Rajmohan Gandhi notes, he was eager to unveil the *Satyagraha* method.[83] The growth of Gandhi's following among India's population was evidenced by the crowds at the dock awaiting his ship.[84] They no longer viewed him as Mohandas Gandhi; he was now referred to as their *Bapu* (Father) and *Mahatma* (Great Soul). The return home provided a much-needed opportunity to evaluate his direction and goal for the struggle ahead.

Gandhi had been living outside of India for nearly two decades and, scholars such as Judith Brown point out, he was feeling the need to return to an obscure existence.[85] He would spend the next year living amongst India's poor to learn and experience societal ills affecting the masses. Large landowners and farmers, usually of British descent, were exploiting indentured laborers across the county. Historians note the existence of a general state of slavery, which ranged from starving children forced to work all day to grown men disfigured from excessive labor.[86] Initially, Gandhi was concerned with finding ways to decrease the suffering among peasants, whether through education or religion,

[81] Dalton, Ibid.
[82] Jagdishchandra Jain, *Gandhi: The Forgotten Mahatma*, (Delhi: K.M. Mittal, Mittal Publications, 1987), 10.
[83] Rajmohan Gandhi, *Gandhi: The Man, His People, and the Empire*, (Berkeley, Calif.: University of California Press, 2007), 173.
[84] Sherrow, Ibid, 60.
[85] Judith Margaret Brown, *Gandhi: Prisoner of Hope*, (Bath, England: Bath Press, 1989), 96.
[86] Wolpert, Ibid, 89.

but the deplorable conditions he encountered required more. With his undying persistence, Gandhi set out to inspire the nation through his teachings of resistance through love.

After returning to India, the opportunity to test his belief in nonviolence presented itself in the small villages of Champaran and Kheda. In 1917, workers and lawyers approached Gandhi about serious injustices against sharecroppers in the respective regions and requested his guidance. They told stories of deplorable and inhuman conditions suffered by laborers at the hands of the British indigo plantation owners. They described landlords who treated workers violently and charged them excessive rent for use of the land they cultivated.[87] It was clear the indentured laborers were virtual slaves to the British.

Unfortunately, as Gandhi would learn, Champaran and Kheda were much like any other Indian villages of their day — marred by poverty, alcoholism and sanitation issues. In March 1918, Gandhi went to Champaran to see for himself the condition of the people and to determine how he could alleviate their suffering. Gandhi, ever optimistic about the potential to help humanity, immediately recognized an opportunity for an agrarian *Satyagraha* campaign.[88]

Upon closer examination of the two areas, Gandhi determined that multiple social ills crippled the population: children were starving and forced to work; women experienced the same degradations imposed upon the poor; and men worked so hard for so little that their bodies were stooped and misshapen from heavy labor.[89] Because these conditions were so widespread, Gandhi realized that he and his supporters could not cure everything at once. He did, however, believe in the combined power of nonviolence and optimism. Bolstered by these principles, Gandhi selected Champaran and Kheda for concurrent *Satyagrahas*.

In Champaran, the landowners had allowed the sharecroppers to use their land in return for a cash crop of indigo, which was used to manufacture a type of blue dye. In the early 1900s, however, the indigo plant was replaced by synthetic dyes, and the price for indigo dropped dramatically. The British landowners taxed the farmers, thus raising the

---

[87] Wolpert, 88.
[88] Fischer, *Gandhi: His Life and Message for the World*. (New York: Mentor Books, 1954), 57.
[89] Wolpert, 89.

rent on the land to compensate for the lost revenue. Clearly, this was a price most sharecroppers could not afford.

Some of the laborers resisted the collection of the tax and were killed for attempting to do so; others had all their possessions seized.[90] Gandhi decided to conduct an investigation, record the sharecroppers' grievances and seek relief from local officials.[91] British landowners tried to disrupt and derail his inquiries at all costs, intimidating some workers and bullying or bribing others. Throughout the entire episode, however, Gandhi's fearlessness and tenacity overcame every obstacle and inspired workers and victims to do the same.

Eventually, the government ordered Gandhi to leave the district because of the disorder he had provoked. After he was arrested, thousands of supporters surrounded the courthouse, and authorities asked Gandhi to help control the crowd.[92] He refused and was brought to trial. Gandhi entered a plea of guilty, but he further explained that he was not disrespectful of the law. He said he simply followed the voice of a higher law — his conscience.[93] The magistrate decided to take some time for reflection before announcing Gandhi's punishment; within days, the case was dropped. Gandhi asserted that this was the first time in India that civil disobedience had triumphed.[94]

Local government officials, at Gandhi's urging, set up an independent commission to address the workers' complaints. Gandhi served on the commission on behalf of the sharecroppers. Just as Gandhi had hoped, the commission found the landowners' system to be a case of "exploitative 'slavery,' " a condition that had existed for nearly a century. They abolished it.[95] The landowners agreed to refund 25 percent of the tax increases already collected.[96] Gandhi's vigilance throughout the Champaran incident was directly tied to the high degree of optimism with which he pursued the end goal, and his positive outlook yielded positive results.

The Kheda agrarian *Satyagraha* occurred simultaneously in another district where sharecroppers paid rent based on crops

---

[90] Sherrow, 62 — 64.
[91] Sherrow, 64.
[92] Fischer, 58.
[93] Fischer, 58.
[94] Fischer, 59.
[95] Wolpert, 89.
[96] Fischer, 59.

produced. The crisis for workers there was caused by a partial crop failure and the government's obstinate attempts to collect full taxes. In early February 1918, Gandhi asked Bombay's governor to suspend revenue payments throughout the entire district until an independent committee could assess the extent of the crop failure. The governor did not object to the assessment, but he also did not commit to suspending revenue collections.[97] Subsequently, he refused to do so. By spring, Gandhi decided to call local peasants into action, and on March 22, 1918, he announced *Satyagraha* at a meeting attended by about 5,000. The struggle continued into early June, but finally ended in compromise: the government agreed to suspend collections from peasants, while rich landowners continued to pay.

These two incidents illustrate Gandhi's basic philosophy and approach to moral values. His efforts were directed at solving a practical problem, not at political expediency. For example, in addition to the grassroots organizing required for a *Satyagraha*, Gandhi spent an equal amount of time and effort creating schools, bringing in medical resources, teaching basic rules of sanitation and improving other areas of a peasant's day-to-day life. One biographer succinctly explained this philosophy:

> The Champaran experience followed a typical Gandhian pattern: it began not as an act of defiance of the British but in an effort to alleviate the misery of the poor. Gandhi's politics grew out of the practical problems of the distressed beings in their day-to-day living. He did not think out his ideas, he worked them out.[98]

It was characteristic of Gandhi to use his optimism to alter the course of his mission as truths evolved and events brought change. One example of this is his attitude toward the British before and after World War I. During the war, Gandhi had cooperated with the British to recruit a large force of India's young men to serve in the military on the side of Britain and its allies. He believed British suggestions that the military

---

[97] Wolpert, 95.
[98] Fischer, 59.

service of approximately 500,000 Indian recruits would earn the country autonomy.[99]

But British attitudes changed. Instead of promoting Indian self-rule, the British became suspicious of independence efforts and attempted to quell any such activities. A commission was charged with studying seditious acts, and its findings led to the controversial Rowlatt Act.[100] This legislation, enacted in 1919, essentially forced martial law upon India, thereby removing normal legal proceedings that protected the accused. The actions appalled many and encouraged Gandhi to call on the Indian population to resist the British. Under Gandhi's leadership, another *Satyagraha* campaign began with the goal of opposing the Rowlatt Act. Additionally, he called for a *hartal*, a national strike of all economic activity.

During the new campaign, in the town of Amritsar, police had issued a proclamation for the roughly 150,000 citizens that forbade meetings and processions. Despite this, protesters planned a demonstration on a plot of empty ground called Jallianwala Bagh. Thousands gathered, and the commanding officer of the town, Brigadier General Reginald E.H. Dyer, placed 25 armed guards on two sides of the crowd. Without warning, the police began to shoot. Gunmen fired 1,650 rounds in about 10 minutes, killing 379 people and wounding 1,137. Dyer said he ordered the shooting because those assembled had ignored his proclamation.[101]

The Jallianwala Bagh incident led to angry outbursts across India. In some areas where the *hartal* was being forged, efforts expanded to include spontaneous acts of violence, such as arson and assaults on English citizens. These acts were grossly contrary to Gandhi's vision, and he abruptly called off the *hartal* on April 18, 1919.[102] Yet this did nothing to erode his belief in India's ability to govern itself, and he still concluded that the nation must separate from British rule, even if that took decades to accomplish.[103]

One step toward a goal of complete independence from Britain, Gandhi felt, was to abolish the salt tax that had been in effect since 1882.

---

[99] Fischer, 60 — 61.
[100] Lawrence James, *Raj: The Making and Unmaking of British Rule.*,(New York: St. Martin's Press, 1997), 468.
[101] Fischer, 65 — 66.
[102] Fischer, 63 — 64.
[103] Sherrow, 67.

The tax required that all salt come from British sources and that residents pay a 2,400 percent tax on the sale price. Gandhi saw this tax as a particularly burdensome regulation because everyone, including the desperately poor, required salt.[104] So at 60 years of age and accompanied by 78 followers, he began a 200-mile, 24-day march from his ashram at Sabarmati to the shores of Dandi, a small village on the coast of Gujarat in western India, to protest the salt tax. Arriving at the seashore, Gandhi broke the law by simply collecting natural salt in defiance of the British monopoly on the collection and distribution of this essential mineral.[105]

The march, in addition to reflecting Gandhi's persistence and discipline, reveals his great understanding of politics and the importance of gaining public awareness and support. He masterfully handled publicity by inviting film crews from around the world. Once again, his cause was not centered on a need for political resistance to Britain, but was grounded in an economic issue: the burden of the salt tax on the poor. Gandhi also grasped the mythological and allegorical elements of the march. One Gandhi authority wrote:

> Whether the allegorical hero was seen as Rama or Buddha, the symbols Gandhi personified were similar: the renunciation of the saint, the valor of the hero, the superior insight of the guru, all combined to symbolize the perfect leader, one who strove earnestly for self-mastery and so might know how to rule the country. "Swaraj (independence) is the only remedy and the way that I have adopted is the only possible way."[106]

The publicity from Gandhi's March to the Sea catapulted the question of Indian autonomy onto the international stage. Britain was seen as a dying empire, guilty of unnecessarily dominating and exploiting the Indian subcontinent for over a century. Gandhi, now frail and old, was seen as the incarnation of nonviolence and love. This juxtaposition inevitably led to an outpouring of support for Gandhi's

---

[104] Wolpert, 143.
[105] Dalton, 91.
[106] Dalton, 108 – 109.

position. It was the last in a lifetime of achievements that demonstrated how — through undying optimism and adherence to ideology — Gandhi was able to overcome the strength of the British Crown.

# THEODORE ROOSEVELT

On a dark night in Milwaukee on October 14, 1912, Theodore Roosevelt stepped up into an open automobile that was to carry him to a public auditorium where he would deliver a campaign speech. The former president and ex-commander of the Rough Riders, who had already served eight years in the White House from 1901 to 1909, was running for an unprecedented third term on the ticket of the independent Progressive Party. The party had been nicknamed the Bull Moose Party after Roosevelt's declaration he was as "healthy as a bull moose."

Suddenly, a shot rang out as the candidate waved to the crowd. There was a violent struggle and shouting beside the open car. Members of the campaign entourage finally subdued a gunman and wrested away a weapon. After someone noticed a bullet hole in the former president's overcoat, Roosevelt looked inside his suit jacket to find the hole went through his vest and shirt. A spreading inkblot of blood just under the candidate's right breast was turning the white shirt crimson.

Despite urgings from his staff to go to the hospital, the wounded Roosevelt declined with this explanation: "I know I am good now; I don't know how long I may be. This may be my last talking this cause to our people, and while I am good I am going to drive to the hall and deliver my speech."[107]

Not only did Roosevelt go to the auditorium where 9,000 people awaited his arrival, but he also delivered every minute of his planned 80-minute speech. The thick stack of paper that contained his rather lengthy remarks most likely helped save his life. The speech, 50 pages long, was folded double and tucked inside his coat pocket. Therefore, the would-be assassin's bullet had to travel through 100 pages of speech text and through an eyeglasses case before causing physical harm. The "lucky" shooting victim believed that the thick speech and hard glasses case decreased the energy of the gunman's fired bullet and likely saved

---

[107] Oliver E. Remey, Henry F. Cochems and Wheeler P. Bloodgood, *The Attempted Assassination of Ex-President Theodore Roosevelt*, (Milwaukee: The Progressive Publishing Company, 1912), 7.

his life.[108] After arriving at the Milwaukee Auditorium, Roosevelt announced to his audience that he had been shot a few minutes earlier, but trivialized the seriousness of the wound, adding: ". . . it takes more than that to kill a bull moose."[109]

Obviously, it was not his last speech. The .38-caliber bullet had lodged in an area that could do no permanent harm, so doctors did not remove the slug. Roosevelt carried it in his body for the rest of his life, apparently without ill effect. For a few days after the shooting, Roosevelt was hospitalized for observation and then released. His assailant, John Flammang Schrank, was examined and found to be mentally incompetent to stand trial, and was sent to the Central State Mental Hospital in Waupun, Wisconsin, where he died in 1943.

Despite Roosevelt's great energy and optimism, the 54-year-old veteran of presidential politics did not win the election of 1912, and he never ran again. In 1901 he had become the country's youngest chief executive at 42 years old when another assassin fatally wounded President William McKinley in the first year of a four-year term. Then McKinley's vice president, Roosevelt served out the rest of the late president's term and won election in his own right in 1904. He did not seek re-election in 1908, which was an option at that time, but he ran as a third-party candidate in 1912. While unsuccessful in that bid, Teddy Roosevelt still secured his place as one of America's most beloved presidents. He even had the famous stuffed toy bear named for him — the "Teddy Bear."[110]

How could one man accomplish so much in life? His biographer, Edmund Morris, points out that Roosevelt created one of the most optimistic images ever impressed upon the American people:

> [H]e left behind a folk consensus that he had been the most powerfully positive American leader since Abraham Lincoln. . . [H]e embodied all America's variety and the whole of its unity. . . what he had made of his own life was possible to all, even to boys born as sickly as himself. Uncounted men, women, and children who had crowded around the

---

[108] Ibid, 9.
[109] Ibid.
[110] Edmund Morris, *Theodore Rex*, (New York: The Modern Library, 2001), 174.

presidential caboose to stare and listen to him now carried, forever etched in memory, the image of his receding grin and wave.[111]

America's 26th president is truly one of this country's most memorable public figures. He encountered enough adventures during his relatively short lifetime for several presidents, politicians, sportsmen, environmentalists and military leaders rolled into one. Various surveys and rankings by modern historians and journalists rank Roosevelt solidly among the top 10 U.S. presidents. A 1999 C-SPAN survey of American historians and experts on the presidency ranked him No. 4 in overall presidential leadership. Ahead of him, listed from top to bottom, were Abraham Lincoln, Franklin Roosevelt and George Washington.[112] A "Survey on Presidents" by the Federalist Society and *Wall Street Journal* ranked Roosevelt No. 5 behind Washington, Lincoln, Franklin Roosevelt and Jefferson. Conducted in 2000, the survey incorporated opinions of 78 scholars in history, political science and law.[113]

It is no wonder the power and energy of this memorable historic figure caught the imagination of America. His list of dangerous escapades and political accomplishments seems endless:

- The force behind the completion of one of the world's largest and most ambitious engineering projects, the Panama Canal
- Spanish-American war hero who organized the Rough Riders and led them in two successful charges during the battle for San Juan Heights in Cuba
- Served as both a vice president and president of the United States
- First American to win a Nobel Prize

---

[111] Ibid, 554 − 555.
[112] C-SPAN Survey of Presidential Leadership, A Site to Complement C-SPAN's 20th Anniversary Television Series, American Presidents: Life Portraits, March-December 1999, www.americanpresidents.org/survey/historians/overall.asp, accessed January 29. 2010.
[113] Federalist Society - The Wall Street Journal Survey on Presidents, www.opinionjournal.com/hail/rankings.html, accessed January 29, 2010.

- First American president to ride in an automobile and fly in an airplane
- Candidate for president on the Bull Moose ticket, a party he founded
- Only third-party presidential candidate to finish in second place ahead of the incumbent president
- New York City police commissioner
- Governor of New York
- Creator of the successful "Big Stick" diplomacy
- First president to invite an African-American to dinner at the White House
- Known as a "trust buster" for attempting to curb the power of large corporations
- One of the first presidents to lead the conservation effort in America
- Hunter, soldier and naturalist who thrived in the outdoors
- Prolific author

Roosevelt's military superiors even nominated him for a Congressional Medal of Honor for his fearless leadership in directing his troops up Kettle Hill in the battle for San Juan Heights in the Spanish-American War. Then-Col. Roosevelt led not only one, but two charges on horseback, fully exposed to withering enemy fire. He would be denied the medal in his lifetime, but was awarded it posthumously by President Bill Clinton just a few days before America's 42nd president left office in January 2001.

His life is proof of the maxim that most great leaders are also great optimists. One would have to be an eternal optimist to tackle and succeed at everything Roosevelt attempted. He expressed a strong belief in the individual and demonstrated a conviction that people can empower themselves to accomplish anything.

In speaking to a class of schoolchildren at Christmas time in Oyster Bay where he made his home, Roosevelt shared his secret for happiness:

> There are two things that I want you to make up your minds to: first, that you are going to have a good time as long as you live — I have no use for the sour-faced

man — and next, that you are going to do something worthwhile, that you are going to work hard and do the things you set out to do.[114]

His definition of optimism included performance and a positive response to defeat and failure. He believed in maintaining the self even in the face of unexpected outcomes. His life reflects a series of transformative events, strung together to yield remarkable outcomes through the purposeful application of idealism, vigor and persistence. These became the former New York governor's brand of unabridged optimism. With this positive mindset as a rulebook, "rough 'n' ready"

Teddy was able to rise to life's challenges, overcome adversity, resist illness and physical disability, and lead a productive, successful personal and political life.[115]

An examination of Roosevelt's early years illustrates the power of optimism to overcome adversity. Young Teddy did not strike most people as promising enough to become one of the nation's greatest presidents.[116] He was born into a privileged and almost aristocratic life in New York City. He could recall watching Abraham Lincoln's funeral procession from an upstairs window of his grandfather's house on Union Square in New York.[117] Despite having the good fortune to be born into a family of wealth and position, Roosevelt was weak and sickly.[118] In the chapter of his autobiography titled "The Vigor of Life," he describes himself as "a sickly boy, with no natural bodily prowess."[119]

Growing up, he suffered from severe asthma, a seriously debilitating condition that was not entirely understood at the time.[120] Fighting for his next breath, "Teedie," as his family was fond of calling

---

[114] Quotations from the Speeches and Other Works of Theodore Roosevelt, The Theodore Roosevelt Association, speech to schoolchildren, Christmastime, Oyster Bay, N.Y., 1898.
[115] James M. Strock, *Theodore Roosevelt on Leadership: Executive Lessons from the Bully Pulpit*, (New York: Three Rivers Press, 2001), 171.
[116] Kathleen Dalton, "The Self-Made Man," Time Magazine, June 25, 2006, www.time.com/time/magazine/article/0,9171,1207796,00.html, accessed January 29, 2010.
[117] Theodore Roosevelt Association, "Timeline: Life of Theodore Roosevelt," www.theodoreroosevelt.org/life/timeline.htm, accessed January 29, 2010.
[118] Dalton, Ibid.
[119] Theodore Roosevelt, *Theodore Roosevelt: An Autobiography*, (New York: McMillan, 1913) Bartleby.com, 1998. Great Books Online, www.bartleby.com/55/. Accessed January 29, 2010.
[120] Dalton, Ibid.

him, often had to sleep propped up in bed or slouching in a chair to obtain relief from his asthma-induced breathing difficulties.[121] Roosevelt's asthma began to overshadow his every activity, and he was deemed "too delicate" for school. As a result, he was privately tutored until he entered college and was often confined indoors and unable to play with other children his age.[122]

To combat the coughing and respiratory problems, doctors prescribed everything from vacations on the coast to smoking cigars to drinking coffee and whiskey.[123] His parents alternately rushed him to seashore resorts and mountain cabins in search of the best air to help him breathe.[124] As he matured, the future champion athlete underwent continuous physical examinations, and his doctors advised him that because of serious heart problems, he should find a desk job and avoid strenuous activity.[125] To many, he seemed unlikely to survive, much less become one of America's most famous and admired presidents. But Roosevelt seemed determined to prove them wrong. For example, when he was 22, anxious physicians cautioned the avid outdoorsman that he had a bad heart and should not even climb stairs. His reaction? He ascended the Matterhorn, Switzerland's tenth-highest peak.[126]

Despite his abundant infirmities and the grim warnings from doctors, Roosevelt's physical body became the cage from which he freed himself. Through his endless supply of crisp optimism, his childhood weakness would turn out to be the provocation for the fierce and robust man he was determined to make himself.

In most great transformations of a human life, there is a precipitating event that brings about the decision to change. Roosevelt's life was no exception. During a visit to see relatives, two boys on the stagecoach bullied and beat him.[127] He was physically unable to defend himself and shocked at the ease with which the two handled him. This event became the catalyst for his determination to build up his body and

---

[121] Nathan Miller, *Theodore Roosevelt: A Life*, (New York: HarperCollins, 1992), 30.
[122] Dalton, Ibid.
[123] Ibid.
[124] Ibid.
[125] H.W. Brands, *TR: The Last Romantic*, (New York: Basic Books, 1997), 49 — 50.
[126] Dalton, Ibid.
[127] Ibid.

learn how to fight.[128] Subsequently, he took up boxing and fought competitively when he was 16, eventually becoming an amateur lightweight champion and later placing second in the Harvard boxing championship during his college days. His interest in the pugilistic art led to similar passions for wrestling, horseback riding, tennis, hiking, rowing, polo and other strenuous athletic endeavors.[129] While he never attained elite success in these sports, he was a passionate athlete and devoted himself to at least two hours of exercise daily for most of his adult life.[130]

Roosevelt's father proved to be a powerful influence on young Teddy's determination to overcome his frailty. At about the time his son reached the end of childhood, the elder Roosevelt insisted on making his favorite child into a strong man by pushing him to embrace a life of vigorous exercise. With characteristic sternness, Theodore Sr. told the boy to throw off his chronic ailments by sheer force of will, ordering him to "make your own body."[131] According to Roosevelt's sister, Anna Roosevelt Cowles, her brother "resolved to make himself strong," to turn his back on his "nervous and timid" childhood and to embrace manhood.[132]

Years later, Roosevelt wrote in his autobiography that his life changed forever because he set fearlessness as the ideal standard that he could achieve through "dogged practice."[133] His optimism apparently fueled an unshakeable confidence in his ability to make changes that would lead to significant improvements. Throughout his life, he maintained an intolerance for weakness, self-degradation and pity. He became a fierce champion of what he called the "strenuous life," a self-imposed struggle to live with vigor and determination.[134] It was a struggle that may, at times, have felt never-ending. From childhood to maturity, he repeatedly injured himself — even sustaining a boxing injury when he was 45 that cost him the sight in his left eye[135] — and

---

128 Ibid.
129 Ibid.
130 SparkNotes, "Theodore Roosevelt, 1880–1884: Entering Manhood and Politics," www.sparknotes.com/biography/troosevelt/section2.rhtml, accessed February 4, 2010.
131 Dalton, Ibid.
132 Ibid.
133 Roosevelt, *An Autobiography*, Ibid, 30.
134 Ibid.
135 Dalton, Ibid.

would variously suffer from polio, asthma, malaria, partial blindness and a weak heart. But he always prevailed, employing nature and exercise to remake his own body.[136] Simply stated, "surrender" had no place in his vocabulary. His focus remained on tapping into personal strength and sustaining a steel-reinforced optimism to shape his life and affect its course.

Even as he grew out of his childhood frailties, Roosevelt was advised by doctors to lead a sedentary life because of lifelong heart and respiratory problems. Of course, he ignored their advice, perhaps most famously in the late 19th century when the future president took command of a ragtag volunteer regiment during the Spanish-American War.[137] This colorful group of misfits and soldiers of fortune, dubbed "The Rough Riders," was made up of volunteer troops recruited from the Western territories and included cowboys, ex-soldiers, Native Americans, lawmen, gun fighters, clergymen, gamblers, gold miners and Ivy League graduates from New York. Together they formed the first U.S. Volunteer Cavalry Regiment.[138]

During the short conflict, Lt. Col. Roosevelt was promoted to colonel and given command of the regiment.[139] Under his leadership, the Rough Riders became famous for dual charges on foot up Kettle Hill and San Juan Heights on July 1, 1898.[140] Of all the Rough Riders, Roosevelt was the only one with a horse, because the troopers' mounts had been left behind due to a lack of transport ships. Roosevelt used the lone horse to ride back and forth between rifle pits at the forefront of the advance up Kettle Hill, an advance that he urged in absence of any orders from superiors. However, he was forced to take the last part of Kettle Hill on foot, due to barbed wire entanglement and a tired mount.[141] His charge up Kettle Hill with a horseless volunteer cavalry unit in the Battle of San Juan Heights proved he had the strength and courage to win a war — even one raging within his own body.[142]

---

136 Ibid.
137 Dalton, Ibid.
138 Theodore Roosevelt, *The Rough Riders*, (New York: Charles Scribner's Sons, 1899), 52.
139 Ibid.
140 Ibid.
141 Ibid.
142 Bill Bleyer, "Medal of Honor Awarded to TR," *Newsday*, January 16, 2001, Theodore Roosevelt Association, www.theodoreroosevelt.org/life/medalofhonor.htm , accessed February 2, 2010.

Roosevelt's willingness to wage a fight in harsh circumstances helped define a certain toughness that would stick with the future president and serve him well in the White House. When he became president in 1901, he combined a love of nature — which dated back to his childhood days, when he collected animal specimens — with his ferocious character. It was a combination that changed the personality of the White House forever.[143]

Within a year of entering politics, he had established a style of his own that he retained throughout his life. He was a reformer as well as an optimist, someone who believed that his own personal standards could effect progress on a global scale. He never hesitated to challenge convention to achieve what he felt was right.[144] For example, he took advantage of what he termed the "bully pulpit" of the presidency to educate voters and legislators about the need for laws to protect natural resources.[145] Roosevelt invented the term, which refers to the power of the office of the presidency as a compelling medium for gaining public attention and support for an issue.[146]

Upon becoming chief executive, Roosevelt used his bully pulpit to tackle an issue that had already defeated one great European country: the building of the 50-mile-long Panama Canal. When France gave up the eight-year project in December 1888, it had cost investors $287 million and 20,000 lives through accidents and disease. Workers had removed 50 million cubic meters of earth and rock but had only dug 11 miles — less than 25 percent of the necessary distance.[147] The French had been defeated by sickness and nature: flooding from the Chagres River, dense rain forest vegetation, poisonous snakes, heat, small pox, yellow fever and malaria. New backers were needed, or the original investors would never be able to recover all of their losses.

The rewards of completion, however, were significant. Once built, the canal would link the Atlantic and Pacific, thereby eliminating the need for the long trip around the tip of South America for all shipping

---

143 Ibid.
144 SparkNotes, Ibid.
145 Dalton, Ibid.
146 C-SPAN Congressional Dictionary, C-SPAN.org, www.c-span.org/guide/congress/glossary/bullypul.htm, accessed February 3, 2010.
147 TR's Legacy—The Panama Canal, *TR: The Story of Theodore Roosevelt*, Public Broadcast System, National Endowment for the Humanities, The American Experience, www.pbs.org/wgbh/amex/tr/panama.html , accessed February 3, 2010.

that traveled from one ocean to the other. The 12,000-mile voyage from New York to San Francisco took months to complete. The same trip using the canal was only about half the distance.

A Frenchman, Ferdinand de Lesseps, had been in charge of the project. He had built the Suez Canal, a 10-year project creating a 119-mile-long sea-level passage linking the Mediterranean Sea and the Red Sea. By joining Europe and Asia, the Suez Canal allowed ships to avoid the time-consuming journey around the tip of Africa. De Lesseps planned to dig a similar sea-level canal across the Isthmus of Panama, an area controlled by Colombia. He estimated the job would cost about $132 million and take 12 years to complete.[148]

U.S. Presidents Ulysses Grant and William McKinley had always been interested in a canal as a military advantage. But it was Roosevelt who acted swiftly and decisively when he saw the opportunity to create a manmade waterway across the Panama Isthmus. When the French gave up their effort, he quickly convinced Congress of the necessity and won approval of a $40 million expenditure to be paid to the French investors for the rights to the canal. In a speech to Congress, Roosevelt said: "No single great material work which remains to be undertaken on this continent is as of such consequence to the American people."[149] But when Colombia was presented with a treaty and offer of $10 million to allow the canal to be built, they rejected it.[150]

But Roosevelt refused to be denied. When Colombia grew reticent in its negotiations, he collaborated with Panamanian business interests on a revolution. The battle for Panama lasted only a few hours. Colombian soldiers in Colón were bribed $50 each to lay down their arms, and the *USS Nashville* cruised off the Panamanian coast in a show of support. On November 3, 1903, the nation of Panama was born.[151]

Not everyone was supportive of Roosevelt's actions, though, as the president himself conceded:

> "There was much accusation about my having acted in an 'unconstitutional' manner," Teddy shrugged. "I took the isthmus, started the canal, and then left

---

[148] Ibid.
[149] TR's Legacy, Ibid.
[150] Ibid.
[151] Ibid.

Congress — not to debate the canal, but to debate me... While the debate goes on, the canal does too; and they are welcome to debate me as long as they wish, provided that we can go on with the canal."[152]

In the first year of its involvement in the canal, the United States fared no better than France had. Three out of four Americans working on the project went home, including the chief engineer. The U.S. government poured $128 million into the project with little to show for it.[153] But with the arrival of John Stevens as the new chief engineer, the situation began to turn around. Congress also approved a new Roosevelt-backed plan that embraced a "lake and lock" approach. Instead of digging a canal at sea level across the isthmus, the plan called for damming a part of the Chagres River to form a large inland lake. A series of locks on each end of the canal would raise vessels to the height of the massive lake. The vessels would then travel across the lake and reaching the other side, be lowered to sea level by another lock.[154]

Stevens also recognized the hazard of swampy land and mosquitoes. So he started a mosquito control program, draining standing water when possible and applying tons of insecticide to other areas. With the improvement in living conditions for workers, illness and death decreased dramatically. Huge steam shovels scooped tons of earth at one time, and railroad cars ran continuously to move the excavated earth where it helped form the Chagres River dam.[155]

Still, the project put the industrial might of America to the test:

> At the Gatun Locks on the Atlantic side, workers poured enough concrete to build a wall 8 feet wide, 12 feet high, and 133 miles long. They built culverts the size of railroad tunnels to channel water from Gatun Lake into the locks. Pittsburgh's furnaces roared as more than fifty mills, foundries, and machine shops

---

[152] J. Buschini, The Panama Canal, President Roosevelt, Small Planet Communications, 2000, www.smplanet.com/imperialism/joining.html, February 3, 2010.
[153] Ibid.
[154] Ibid.
[155] Ibid.

churned out the rivets, nuts and bolts, girders, and other steel pieces the canal builders needed.[156]

By May 1913, engineers were preparing to test the canal and locks system. On September 26, a tugboat traveled through the locks and onto the newly formed Lake Gatun. The canal and locks worked flawlessly, and the Panama Canal opened officially on August 15, 1914. But the world scarcely noticed. "German troops were driving across Belgium toward Paris; the newspapers relegated Panama to their back pages. The greatest engineering project in the history of the world had been dwarfed by the totality of World War I."[157]

Lack of global recognition aside, however, Teddy Roosevelt's vision and optimism had resulted in a great achievement for the United States. The project was not only a stunning engineering feat, but it also achieved a public health breakthrough: yellow fever was completely and permanently wiped out on the isthmus, with the last case reported in Panama City on November 11, 1905.[158] But the cost to America was significant: about 5,600 workers lost their lives due to illness and accidents and $375 million was spent. The canal was the single most expensive construction project in U.S. history to that time — even though it actually was completed at a cost that was $23 million less than estimated in 1907.[159]

Each one of the three chief engineers has been credited at one time or another with making the Panama Canal a reality. Presidents Woodrow Wilson and William Howard Taft also have shared credit because the construction period encompassed their administrations. Taft took an avid interest in the project and visited the construction site on several occasions, and the canal opened during Wilson's term. But the last chief engineer of the project, Col. George Washington Goethals, credited another president. "The real builder of the Panama Canal," he said, "was Theodore Roosevelt."[160]

---

[156] Ibid.
[157] Ibid.
[158] A History of the Panama Canal— French and American Construction Efforts: Prepared by the Panama Canal Authority Technical Resources Center and Corporate Communications Division,
www.pancanal.com/eng/history/history/index.html, accessed February 3, 2010.
[159] Ibid.
[160] TR's Legacy, Ibid.

Roosevelt, a living symbol of America's industrial age, was an executive who could get things done. And while the Panama Canal may have been a testimony to his expertise in the art of political persuasion, the roots of those skills dated back to his earlier days in New York, where Roosevelt's engaging personality, endless energy and abundance of optimism laid the foundation for a life that would extend to the White House and beyond.

A little more than a year after he graduated from Harvard — and while still attending law school at Columbia — Roosevelt became the youngest man elected to the New York State Assembly. He also served as the Republican minority leader in the statehouse. As minority leader, he sought reforms for conservation, stemming from his great love of the outdoors.[161] Discovering both an affinity and a talent for politics, Roosevelt dropped out of law school in 1882 after two years of study. He was re-elected to the New York assembly by the widest margin of any representative from New York City. In 1882 he also published his first book, the acclaimed *The Naval War of 1812*, which set the standard for studies on naval strategy and was required reading at the Naval Academy in Annapolis for many years.[162] A prolific writer, his more than three-dozen books also included titles such as, *Hunting Trips of a Ranchman, Life of Thomas Hart Benton, Life of Gouverneur Morris, Ranch Life and the Hunting Trail, Essays in Practical Politics, The Winning of the West* (four volumes) and *The Wilderness Hunter*.[163]

As many of these titles indicate, Roosevelt was always interested in the outdoors, hunting and preserving the sportsman's way of life. His interests broadened to include resources that were of strategic interest to an early industrial age America. As president, Roosevelt joined forces with a close friend and forester, Gifford Pinchot, in warning the public that the natural resources of the United States were not inexhaustible; that a timber famine was imminent; and that coal, iron and oil and gas reserves would run out some day.

Congressional leaders did not, however, want to hear about game or tree protection or about the resource needs of future generations. But the president regarded the nation's trees, open land and animal inhabitants as prime constituencies whose interests he must serve and

---

161 SparkNotes, Ibid.
162 Theodore Roosevelt Association, Ibid.
163 Smithsonian, Ibid.

protect.[164] In an August 6, 1912, address to the Progressive National Convention in Chicago, he stated: "There can be no greater issue than that of conservation in this country."[165]

There were few effective conservation plans at the turn of the 20th century,[166] which made Roosevelt's philosophies groundbreaking. At the time, the idea of conserving the land primarily meant saving it for later use by future generations, not preservation of areas of land without intrusion or interference of man.[167] For this reason, most of the conserved land at that point was forest that provided valuable timber.[168] Roosevelt disagreed with that concept, telling the nation, "We are prone to speak of the resources of this country as inexhaustible; this is not so."[169] He underscored his commitment to the land by associating himself with many prominent conservationists of the time, including Pinchot and John Muir, a naturalist and founder of the Sierra Club.

In the spring of 1903, he used a trip to the American West to dramatize his commitment to preserving wild places.[170] Traveling to Yosemite and Yellowstone, Teddy saw first hand the depletion of natural resources as well as the untouched natural beauty still in need of protection.[171] He observed the Grand Canyon, the giant sequoia and redwood trees in the fern forest of the Pacific Northwest and the rugged span of the Badlands.[172] After having toured the nation on several campaign trips, the exuberant lover of wild America was determined to conserve as much land as possible.[173]

In a speech at Osawatomie, Kansas, on August 31, 1910, Roosevelt outlined his views on conservation of the lands of the United States:

---

[164] Dalton, Ibid.
[165] Theodore Roosevelt Association, Ibid.
[166] C.M. Shorter, "Theodore Roosevelt — Legacy of a Conservation Leader," online article Tigerhomes.com, www.tigerhomes.org/animal/theodore-Roosevelt.cfm, 2006, accessed February 1, 2010.
[167] SparkNotes, Ibid.
[168] Theodore Roosevelt, "The Conservation of Natural Resources," from "Theodore Roosevelt's Seventh Annual Message to Congress," December 3, 1907, Public Broadcast System, "New Perspectives on the West," Archives of the West, The West Film Project, 2001, www.pbs.org/weta/thewest/resources/archives/eight/trconserv.htm, accessed February 1, 2010.
[169] SparkNotes, Ibid.
[170] Dalton, Ibid.
[171] Shorter, Ibid.
[172] Ibid.
[173] SparkNotes, Ibid.

Conservation means development as much as it does protection. I recognize the right and duty of this generation to develop and use the natural resources of our land but I do not recognize the right to waste them, or to rob, by wasteful use, the generations that come after us.

... Moreover, I believe that the natural resources must be used for the benefit of all our people, and not monopolized for the benefit of the few, and here again is another case in which I am accused of taking a revolutionary attitude... Now, with the water-power, with the forests, with the mines, we are brought face to face with the fact that there are many people who will go with us in conserving the resources only if they are to be allowed to exploit them for their benefit. That is one of the fundamental reasons why the special interests should be driven out of politics.

... Of all the questions which can come before this nation, short of the actual preservation of its existence in a great war, there is none which compares in importance with the great central task of leaving this land even a better land for our descendants than it is for us, and training them into a better race to inhabit the land and pass it on. Conservation is a great moral issue, for it involves the patriotic duty of insuring the safety and continuance of the nation.[174]

Thus the naturalist, hunter and Rough Rider became one of the greatest conservation icons of the 20th century. His administration protected more federal land than that of any other president.[175] Protected national forests acreage increased from just over 40 million acres to almost 200 million under his conservation stewardship. At the time of his inauguration in 1901, there were only five national parks in

---

174 Morris, Ibid, 54.
175 Shorter, Ibid.

the United States; Roosevelt not only added land to those parks, but also authorized legislation to create five more.[176] He added government protection to the national forests in the West, reserved lands for public use and initiated large irrigation projects.[177] During his two administrations, Roosevelt purchased 150 million acres of land for forest reserves, organized the National Forest Service,[178] and placed 230 million acres of U.S. land under public protection from development.[179]

Roosevelt's optimism about conservation was an "active optimism" — the unbridled belief that nothing was impossible, marked by a willingness to work or do whatever it takes to make a goal, or even a dream, come true. To his way of thinking, the problem of America's dwindling natural resources could be averted through protective, proactive measures. So he acted, confident in his optimistic view that responsible efforts would yield effective results.

For all his ruggedness and interest in guns, hunting and military action, Roosevelt also proved to be an effective mediator and peacemaker. Using his powers of persuasion, he was able to get Russian and Japanese negotiators to the bargaining table to discuss ending the Russo-Japanese War, which began in 1904.[180] A root cause of the conflict was the ambition of both Russia and Japan to expand their respective sphere of influence in the Far East. Russia also wanted a second warm water port that provided access to areas of China, Korea and Japan. The Russians devised a partial solution to their quest for a second warm water port by leasing Port Arthur, located on the Liáodōng Peninsula of Manchuria, from the Chinese.[181]

Hostilities began on February 8, 1904, with a surprise attack on Port Arthur by the Japanese without first issuing a formal declaration of war. (The tactic would be repeated on the American naval base at Pearl Harbor on December 7, 1941, to bring America into World War II.) Port Arthur remained under siege until January 2, 1905, when the

---

[176] Ibid.
[177] Ibid.
[178] SparkNotes, Ibid.
[179] John Morton Blum, "Theodore Roosevelt: the Bully Pulpit," 2002, Essay, National Video Resources, 73 Spring Street, Suite 403, New York, NY 10012, www.nvr.org/pres_content.php?pro=pres&sec=essay&subsec=1, accessed February 4, 2010.
[180] The Russo-Japanese War Society, "Introduction," russojapanesewar.com, www.russojapanesewar.com/intro.html, 2002, accessed January 29, 2010.
[181] Ibid.

commander of the garrison surprised the Japanese by surrendering. Then, in the battle of Tsu Shima on May 27, 1905, the Japanese fleet annihilated the Russian Baltic fleet. The Japanese, launching a hail of naval artillery shells at the rate of 2,000 per minute, sank 22 Russian vessels—including four new battleships—captured seven ships, and killed 4,000 Russian personnel in the process. The Japanese lost only three torpedo boats.[182]

Roosevelt intervened to bring the dispute to mediation before both countries suffered further losses of property and human life. He believed that if fighting continued, Russia would lose all her holdings in the Far East and change the region's balance of power in a way that was detrimental to U.S. interests. Ever the optimist, he also believed he was the one who could help bring the war to an end, so he summoned representatives of the two warring countries to Portsmouth, New Hampshire, where negotiators ultimately reached a peace treaty. For his efforts, Theodore Roosevelt won a Nobel Peace Prize, the first Nobel Prize awarded to an American.

According to Roosevelt biographer Edmund Morris, the president's accomplishment was in no small part due to sheer force of will:

> The peace the President had made possible at Portsmouth was the result of just such an inexplicable ability to impose his singular charge upon plural power. By sheer force of moral purpose, by clarity of perception, by mastery of detail and benign manipulation of men, he had become, as Henry Adams admiringly wrote him, "the best herder of Emperors since Napoleon."[183]

Peacemaking, however, was not an unfamiliar role for the president. He had already earned a reputation as an effective mediator among conflicting nations even before the Russo-Japanese War. His diplomatic philosophy was encapsulated in a West African proverb he enjoyed quoting: "Speak softly but carry a big stick. You will go far."[184]

---

[182] Morris, Ibid, 387.
[183] Morris, Ibid, 414.
[184] Theodore Roosevelt, "Letter to Henry L. Sprague," Albany, N.Y., January 26, 1900, American Treasures of the Library of Congress, A gift of the heirs of Theodore Roosevelt Jr., www.loc.gov/exhibits/treasures/trm139.html, accessed February 2, 2010.

Interestingly, Roosevelt first used the proverb not as a world leader, but as governor of New York in reference to a dispute with one of the state's powerful political bosses. Later in his dealings with other international powers, he used the proverb to suggest that a nation that appears strong and ready to act often causes opponents to back down without warfare.[185]

Roosevelt used his Big Stick Diplomacy — as the press called it — to settle a 1902 dispute between Venezuela and Germany in which the South American nation defaulted on repayment of a loan to the European power. Germany blockaded the country to force payment, and Roosevelt threatened to remove the blockade by military force, if necessary. But the president's motives were as pragmatic as they were peaceful. He believed the Germans were attempting to get a toehold in South America in defiance of the 1823 Monroe Doctrine, which declared that European nations were forbidden to further colonize any South American nation.[186] So he articulated a policy that became known as the Roosevelt Corollary, which made it clear that the United States would use force to prevent further European influence in Latin America. Roosevelt declared, "We cannot afford to let Europe get a foothold in our backyard, so we'll have to act as policemen for the West."[187] Ultimately, the Germans backed down, and the two countries negotiated for a year before reaching a peaceful agreement.

America's 26th President was not afraid to wield that same kind of influence domestically, either. For example, rather than simply maintaining the status quo, he sought a mid-course political path between Republican-based economic liberalism and the socialism advocated by some reformers. He even attempted to move the Republican Party in the direction of change and reform, including breaking up corporate monopolies and increasing regulation of businesses.

Referring to the relationship between the working class and large corporations, Roosevelt invented what he called the "Square Deal." In a speech to attendees of the New York State Fair in Syracuse on September 7, 1903, he explained the meaning of the Square Deal:

---

[185] Miller, 337.
[186] "Venezuela Crisis 1902," Military, GlobalSecurity.org, www.globalsecurity.org/military/ops/venezuela1902.htm, accessed February 4, 2010.
[187] Ibid.

Let the watchwords of all our people be the old familiar watchwords of honesty, decency, fair-dealing, and commonsense... We must treat each man on his worth and merits as a man. We must see that each is given a square deal, because he is entitled to no more and should receive no less... The welfare of each of us is dependent fundamentally upon the welfare of all of us.[188]

Roosevelt's tendency to swim against the currents — political, economic, international or otherwise — required him to maintain a tough mind and equally hard-shell exterior. He had managed to do just that, never admitting weakness or showing frailty, living life to the fullest by "constantly forcing himself to do the difficult and even dangerous thing."[189] He continued to do so after leaving politics, notably in an expedition to South America. On this occasion, however, the challenges would eventually prove too great for even a person of Roosevelt's courage and stamina.

Near the end of his last term as president, Roosevelt had been constantly petitioned by an old friend and aspiring explorer, Father John Zahm, to join him on a South American river adventure. Sponsored by the American Museum of Natural History, Roosevelt finally agreed, venturing into the Brazilian jungle in 1913 and journeying down the dangerous and unmapped River of Doubt — which was later renamed Rio Roosevelt in his honor.[190]

Unfortunately, the president's group was ill-prepared for such an expedition, racing against time before both food and supplies ran out. Throughout the trip, he and his team—including his son, Kermit — faced and overcame the perils of land and water, including ferocious animals and hostile natives.[191] Roosevelt contracted malaria and a serious infection resulting from a minor leg wound. The infection caused severe illness, chest pain, fever and delirium. Six weeks into the adventure, he

---

[188] Theodore Roosevelt Association, Ibid.
[189] Dalton, Ibid.
[190] William Roscoe Thayer, *Theodore Roosevelt: An Intimate Biography,* (Boston: Houghton Mifflin, 1919), 4 – 7, Bartleby.com: Great Books Online, 2000, www.bartleby.com/170/23.html, accessed February 1, 2010.
[191] Ibid.

lay at death's door and had to be attended day and night by the expedition's physician.[192] Tragically, Roosevelt's body seemed to be returning to the weak, debilitated condition of his childhood. He considered his own state a threat to the survival of other expedition members and bravely volunteered to be left behind so the remaining rations could be used to save the others. His son Kermit would not allow it.

But once again, the tough cavalry officer somehow pulled through. However, the effects of the South America journey weakened him and significantly contributed to his declining health.[193] For the rest of his life, Roosevelt would be plagued by flare-ups of malaria and leg inflammations so severe that he would require hospitalization.[194] On January 6, 1919, nearly five years after the expedition, one of the country's greatest presidents would die at home in his sleep from a heart attack. He was only 60 years old. The trip to Brazil took such a physical toll that Roosevelt never fully recovered. His health issues were further exacerbated by the tremendous emotional loss following the death of his youngest son, Quentin, a combat pilot shot down July 14, 1918, behind German lines during World War I.[195]

Roosevelt's personal voyage from asthmatic patient to hearty hunter, rancher, explorer, naturalist and world leader reflects a broader vision for the office of president. In many ways, his personal brand of optimism — buoyant and assured, and always underscored by a toughness that was honed by a childhood of fragile health and a refusal to be anything less than he could be — became a kind of political tool that defined the man and his achievements. Author James Strock perhaps said it best:

> Even now, seeing his faded photograph, one senses
> Roosevelt's vitalized optimism. Having declared that
> the future of the nation depended on the character of
> its citizens, TR said he was optimistic about both. He
> decried those early investigative journalists he termed

192 Ibid.

193 Ibid.

194 Ibid.

195 *New York Times* obituary, "Theodore Roosevelt," January 6, 1919, Theodore Roosevelt Association, www.theodoreRoosevelt.org/life/NYTobit.htm, accessed February 1, 2010.

"muckrakers," who focused almost entirely on what was wrong and dispiriting, rather than what was good and inspiring. As he said of democracy, one should join those who "try to make the best of it," avoiding those who "always see the worst of it."[196]

Theodore Roosevelt did, indeed, always try to "make the best of it." In doing so, he left a better America for every generation that followed.

---

[196] Ibid, 171.

# NELSON MANDELA

In 1942, while working in a law office in racially segregated South Africa, a minor incident involving a simple teacup left an indelible mark upon 24-year-old Nelson Mandela. It was an experience that would forever shape his vision and destiny. Twenty-two years later, Mandela wrote about his first teatime at the all-white Johannesburg law firm:

> On my first day at the office the white senior typist said, "Look, Nelson, we have no color bar here. When the tea-boy brings the tea, come and get yours from the tray. We have brought two new cups for you and Gaur Radike — another African employee. You must use them. Tell Gaur about your cups. Be careful of him, Nelson, he is a bad influence." I duly told Gaur, whose response was, "I will show you. Do exactly as I do." When the tea arrived, Gaur boycotted the new cups and picked one of the old ones. I had no desire to quarrel with him or the senior typist, so for months I did not drink tea.[197]

The incident is telling in three respects. First, it shows the extent of the bigotry by the white employees, who provided the two young African men with easily identifiable cups of their own. That way, the white employees would not drink from the same cups as the Africans. Second, it reveals the hypocrisy of an apartheid system. The white office typist ignored the open racial discrimination, stating that "we have no color bar here." The discrimination was open and obvious. Racial equality was but a great and unspoken illusion. And third, it demonstrates Mandela's intention to avoid conflict and seek peace. Instead of upsetting one party or the other by selecting a cup, he chose simply not to drink tea.

Therefore, it is surprising that as a young man, Nelson Mandela left his life of relative comfort and privilege to spearhead the movement for

---

[197] Nelson Mandela, "An Autobiographical Note by Nelson Mandela, 1964," South African History Online, www.sahistory.org.za/pages/library-resources/articles_papers/1960s-auto-mandela.html , accessed November 24, 2009.

racial and political equality in apartheid-entrenched South Africa. The same deep sense of unyielding principle and integrity that drew Mandela to social activism also fueled his lifelong commitment to achieving a multiracial democracy. Despite personal tragedy, grave political concessions and a prison sentence that kept him from his family, friends and loved ones for almost three decades, Mandela never wavered from his mission or doubted he would succeed.

By examining Mandela's path and the commitment that guided it, we begin to understand how the restructuring of a nation began, simply enough, from the dogged resilience of a single optimistic man. Well into his 90s, Mandela has practiced an active optimism, leading mass demonstrations, holding secret meetings with former foes and playing an unquestionably pivotal role in unifying a nation that has become an exemplary international model of conflict resolution and consensus building.

The fine, papery lines that now cross Mandela's nonagenarian face betray a life of immense sacrifice and principle. His work has garnered the 1993 Nobel Peace Prize, which he shared with one of his greatest political foes, Frederik Willem de Klerk, the last president of apartheid-era South Africa. And while Mandela's accomplishments have earned him prestigious accolades in the same halls of white privilege that once demonized the anti-apartheid movement, they have also cost him two marriages and robbed him of the ethereal joy in holding his children for the 27 years of his imprisonment. Yet, Nelson Mandela has taken, and continues to take, responsibility for each aspect of his life. As his story reveals, his choices throughout life are clinical, strategic and unrelentingly optimistic, dedicated to bringing his visions to reality.

Quoting from W.E. Henley's poem "Invictus," Mandela often states, "I am the master of my fate; I am the captain of my soul."[198] Optimism has enabled him to embody this self-fulfilling mentality. Optimism in this sense is neither simple nor passive. It is an active tool that Mandela uses to create the world he wants to see. Whether it is defining his own image as a symbol in the media or connecting on a human level to break political barriers, Mandela's own optimism and perseverance served as both a symbol and guiding beacon of the struggle for a people to achieve justice and equality.

---

[198] William Ernest Henley, "Invictus," *Best Loved Poems of the American People*, ed. Hazel Felleman, (New York: Doubleday, 1936), 73.

His story begins in the vast and mountainous Transkei region of South Africa that lies in the lower rim of the country, cupped between Lesotho and the Indian Sea. It is here that Rohlihlahla, or Nelson Mandela, was born in the summer of 1918. For centuries, 12 tribes belonging to the Xhosa-speaking people governed the region's societal affairs and commerce. The Xhosa conducted a democratic society with relatively egalitarian structures to administer communal justice and debate. The tribal members subsisted through maize-based agriculture, sheep and cattle herding and trade. The Xhosa had existed relatively untouched by rapidly expanding British control in South Africa.[199]

By the mid-19th century, however, just 60 years before Mandela's birth, the Xhosa began to feel the effects of Britain's tightening grip on the Transkei, one of two major tribal reserve areas designated by the British. Like the Dutch-descended Afrikaner populations before them, the Xhosa were barraged with increasingly disruptive measures that included redistribution of land wealth and the weakening of tribal chiefdoms and legal structure. Authorities also required Xhosa people to acquire British names and limit the use of their native languages.[200] Finally, after their eighth war with British forces, the Xhosa lost full autonomy and suffered a tumultuous period of starvation and disenfranchisement. The tribal chiefs, whose stories of honor and elite military prowess surrounded Mandela in his childhood, were disgraced and imprisoned on a former leper colony off the coast of Cape Town. It was called Robben Island. And it would eventually become the place of imprisonment for Nelson Mandela.

Decades later, Mandela's childhood as an elite member of the Tembu tribe was an idyllic one.[201] The Transkei was beautifully rural, and Mandela often recounted his love for it during his imprisonment.[202] His grandfather, King Ngubengcuka, was a great Tembu ruler who died prior to the British control of Tembuland, located in the Transkei. Young Mandela felt empowered throughout life by the fact that he was descended from a tribal chief. While he did not display a sense of entitlement, Mandela and his family were accustomed to being treated with utmost respect. A classmate of Mandela's would later state:

---

[199] Anthony Sampson, *Mandela: The Authorized Biography*, (New York: Alfred A. Knopp, 1999), 26.
[200] Ibid, 9.
[201] Ibid, 8.
[202] Ibid.

Xhosa princes think the world belongs to them. . . .
Some would kick tribesman out of their way, thinking
everyone else is unimportant. Aristocrats can't believe
you'll contradict them — as in Britain, like the women
in Harrods who ignore everyone else and say loudly:
"I'll have some of that." Mandela never displayed that
arrogance, and always respected commoners. . . who
were cleverer than he; but he became accustomed to
people treating him like a prince.[203]

Mandela's family, including his father and several brothers and
sisters, lived in four self-sufficient *kraals*, each one belonging to one of
Mandela's four "mothers." Each *kraal* (a village of huts) consisted of
several *rondavels*, or circular huts for sleeping cooking and gathering.
The Xhosa language does not discriminate between half- or step-
relations, and each of his father's wives was considered Mandela's
"mother" and shared parenting and subsistence responsibilities.[204]

Mandela's father Hendry was a nobleman who had been
dispossessed of much of his wealth by a local white magistrate. Still,
Mandela and his family enjoyed a privileged status in their community.
According to biographer and friend Anthony Sampson: "Hendry
Mandela was a strict father with a stubbornness (Mandela) suspects he
inherited. . . . He was illiterate, pagan, and polygamous; he was tall and
dignified. . . with no sense of inferiority toward whites. He inhabited a
self contained world with its own customs and traditions."[205] In 1927,
when Rohlihlahla was just 9 years old, Hendry died from a pulmonary
disease. Sensing that Nelson had a promising mind, he had asked his
friend and political ally Jongintaba to raise and educate the youth.

Jongintaba was Regent and acting king of the Tembu tribe and lived
in a tribal center far more metropolitan than the village of Mandela's
birth. Mandela excelled in his studies at a local mission school, enjoyed
horseback riding and admired Jongintaba's sense of style and way of
conducting court.[206] He also learned important lessons about leadership
from the Regent. Jongintaba emphasized the political importance of

---

203 Ibid, 26.
204 Ibid, 7.
205 Ibid, 6.
206 Ibid, 11.

using persuasion to unify people and mollify factionalism. "If one or two animals stray, you go out and draw them back to the flock," he said. "That's an important lesson in politics." More than 60 years later, Mandela would use these skills to avert a civil war in South Africa and bring about the multiracial democracy of which he dreamed.

Mandela's education was further enriched by mentorship and knowledge of oral histories provided by visiting chiefs and noblemen. These stories shared the core African values and proud history of the Xhosa as a unified and successful people.[207] One such value was *ubuntu*, which refers to a sense of brotherhood and mutual responsibility that human beings are meant to show for one another.[208] This optimistic vision of a unified and empowered African citizenry guided Mandela throughout his life, and he invoked this principle repeatedly in his speeches.

While his birth name was Rohlihlahla, or "troublemaker," in boarding school Mandela was given the English name Nelson. However, it seems that the meaning of his Xhosa name stuck even before he had committed to political activism as an adult.

South Africa was ruled by a white minority. Segregation was an informal way of life until 1948 when *apartheid* laws were enacted, institutionalizing racial discrimination. In 1943, Mandela joined the African National Congress (ANC), an organization originally founded to increase the rights of the black South African population. The next year he and his future law partner, Oliver Tambo, and Walter Sislu (Mandela's mentor and lifelong friend) were instrumental in creating the ANC Youth League. The Youth League aimed to involve the masses of people in militant struggles.[209]

When Mandela entered the ANC as a young man, he believed he would one day become the center of the organization.[210] As he revealed to astonished listeners as president of the ANC Youth League, he even held the idea that he would one day serve as the first non-white president of South Africa.[211] This sense of his personal future was

---

[207] Ibid, 12.
[208] Ibid.
[209] African National Congress Youth League official Web site (http://www.ancyouthleague.org/home/index.php?option=com_content&view=article&id=47 ), accessed December 3, 2009.
[210] Sampson, 69.
[211] James Champy and Nitin Norhia, *The Arc of Ambition: Defining the Leadership Journey*, (New York: Perseus Books Group, 1999), 56.

coupled with a keen attention to the power of political seduction, and Mandela's carefully cultivated appearance played no small part in the development of both. Throughout his life, Mandela was sensitive to how he wanted to be perceived and took care to dress accordingly. As a child living in the Regent's home, he took notice of his father figure's style and resolved to always be well-dressed.[212] As a young man, he prided himself on his boxer's physique, and often posed shirtless for the camera in various boxing poses. He wore flashy suits and colors that, with his increasingly self-confident smile and charm, made him popular among women and gave him a reputation as an unequivocal ladies' man.[213] This awareness of his image would later allow him to control and define his role as an increasingly powerful political symbol — another way in which he actively defined his destiny.

In 1952, Mandela and others were arrested, charged under the Suppression of Communism Act and given a suspended prison sentence. Later that same year, he was elected deputy national president of the ANC. Further alleged subversive activities led to a treason charge in 1956 that included 155 other activists; they were all acquitted after a four-year trial.

One of the most tragic events of political protest in modern South African history occurred in 1960 as members of the Pan Africanist Congress (PAC), another organization formed to resist apartheid, assembled a group of protestors in Sharpeville to oppose "pass" laws. These laws required blacks to carry identification papers similar to an international passport used by world travelers; their intent was to limit the travel of blacks within their homeland. The passes were among the most hated symbols of apartheid, highlighting the widespread segregation, white attitudes about racial inferiority and cruel acts borne by white domination.[214] While the ANC and PAC planned peaceful protests, a PAC demonstration at Sharpeville ended in tragedy when police, unnerved by the size of the crowd, fired live ammunition point blank into the gathering of unarmed men, women and children. An estimated 69 civilians were killed and nearly 200 injured. The white apartheid government banned both the ANC and PAC.

---

[212] Sampson, Ibid, 10.
[213] Ibid, 37.
[214] C.G. Weeramantry, *Justice without Frontiers: Furthering Human Rights*, (Cambridge, MA: Kluwer Law International, 1997), 375.

By this time, Mandela had lost faith in the efficacy of peaceful demonstrations to end apartheid and bring racial justice to South Africa. He created a military group and even traveled outside the country for training in terrorist and military tactics. Using disguises and keeping out of sight, Mandela lived "underground" for more than a year. He was finally arrested in 1962 for his activities, convicted and sentenced to five years in prison. While serving the sentence on Robben Island, a former leper colony and mental asylum, Mandela and other members of the ANC were charged again with treason. They were convicted and faced possible death by hanging, but the judge handed down a life sentence. In the winter of 1964, Mandela and his co-defendants were packed off to Robben Island, located off the tip of Cape Town.

Mandela's optimism and positive outlook enabled him to survive 27 years in prison, eventually leave his confinement and return to public life the conquering hero. From the start, he refused to be intimidated by guards. When one became enraged and threatened to hit him, Mandela said, "If you so much as lay a hand on me, I will take you to the highest court in the land. And when I finish with you, you will be as poor as a church mouse." The guard went away without carrying through on his threat.[215]

Mandela also presented the utmost perception of gentlemanliness, treating everyone like royalty. For example, two months after he was incarcerated at Robben Island, his lawyer, George Bizos, came to see him in prison. Mandela was escorted to the visitation room by eight guards who formed a box around him. Mandela and Bizos chatted briefly, and then Mandela said: "George, I'm sorry, I have not introduced you to my guard of honor." He then introduced his guards to Bizos by name. The guards were so surprised by Mandela's action that each one shook hands politely with Bizos and acted as though they actually were an honor guard.[216]

Mandela's optimism allowed him to see every situation as an opportunity. This characteristic is an important one in overcoming tremendous challenges—the awareness that every engagement is an opportunity. He made the most of his many endless hours in prison by reading, studying and discussing topics with his fellow activists. They

---

[215] John Carlin, *Playing the Enemy: Nelson Mandela and the Game that Made a Nation*, (New York: The Penguin Group, 2008), 30.
[216] Ibid, 29 — 30.

called prison "the university." Mandela always took the long view of matters. What happened in the long run was more important, he believed, than the short-term approach. He always kept his eye on the distant goal,[217] learning things that would serve his ultimate ambition: to become the first president of a free Republic of South Africa. For example, he became fluent in Afrikaans, an Indo-European language derived from Dutch that was spoken in South Africa. He used this skill to talk to his Boer jailers in a language they were more comfortable speaking. By learning the language of his opposition, Mandela also demonstrated his sincerity in creating an inclusive society in which all cultures were welcomed and appreciated.

The greatest change in Nelson Mandela, however, was a mellowing of his temperament from firebrand activist and military leader to a pacifist who considered all points of view in his politics. He realized that violence would not solve South Africa's problems. He knew that his job was to win over his opponents to his side. The ANC did not have enough military resources to go to war and defeat the Afrikaners. Their struggle could only be won by negotiations.[218]

So Mandela immediately set about learning all he could about the Afrikaner's mind and psychology. He used that information to make friends with his guards, seeking insight as to their interests. He then researched these topics so he could make small talk with his warders about subjects they were passionate about — which included rugby, a fact that would play an important role in South Africa's future. In studying the Afrikaners, Mandela saw similarities between whites and blacks. During conversations with Afrikaners, he pointed out that both whites and blacks had struggled for freedom. The Boers fought with the British to hold on to their land. Mandela also praised the character of the Boers, who he saw as straightforward but also soft-hearted to those in need.

In 1985, a unique opportunity for rapprochement with the white leaders presented itself to Mandela. Doctors discovered he had an enlarged prostate that would require surgery. He underwent the surgery, which was successful, but required weeks of recovery in the hospital. It was the first time he had been allowed to live outside a jail

---

[217] Ibid, 57.
[218] Ibid, 21.

70

cell in 23 years,[219] and he saw this as an opportunity to woo white South Africa. Mandela's optimism buoyed his efforts to meet secretly with government officials and win over hard-core Afrikaners who had been fighting and killing ANC activists for decades.[220] He first sought a meeting with the country's minister of justice, Kobie Coetsee, who also administered the prison system. When they met, Mandela turned on the charm, creating a strong positive impression for Coetsee.

> "He was a natural," Coetsee recalled, sparkling with animation, "and I realized that from the moment I set eyes on him. He was a born leader. And he was affable. He was obviously well liked by the hospital personnel and yet he was respected, even though they knew that he was a prisoner. And he was clearly in command of his surroundings."[221]

Coetsee also said he was impressed by Mandela's willingness to speak in Afrikaans and by his thorough understanding of Afrikaans history.

Those impressions aside, the main concern of Coetsee and South African President P.W. Botha was the present. In the 1980s, violence had grown appreciably on both sides. There was fighting among blacks, mainly between anti-apartheid groups and right-wing factions who were willing to work with the current oppressive regime. A publicity campaign outside South Africa turned the world's attention to Mandela's plight. This publicity eventually led to boycotts of South Africa; other countries, such as the United States, declined to do business with the South African government. Both white and black South Africans feared that the apartheid struggle would end in violence. A national poll conducted in the summer of 1985 showed that 70 percent of the black population and 30 percent of the whites believed that the country was headed toward a civil war.[222]

To help facilitate talks, Botha had Mandela transferred to Pollsmoor Prison, a maximum-security facility located in a suburb of Cape Town.

---

[219] Ibid, 24.
[220] Ibid, 20 — 21.
[221] Ibid, 24.
[222] Ibid, 20.

Though kept in an isolated part of the prison, Mandela was being groomed for release back into civilian life. He was taken on drives and allowed to stroll free on public streets. He even visited the home of one of his jailers with whom he had become friends. Once, authorities took him to a beach on the Atlantic Ocean where he walked alone in the sand. By observing Mandela's behavior, Coetsee decided that the former revolutionary had mellowed and would not take a vengeful attitude toward whites once he was freed.[223]

Botha, however, was ultimately the audience Mandela sought. He decided he must go through the man guarding the presidential door, Niel Barnard, head of the National Intelligence Service. Barnard was interested in learning from Mandela whether it was possible to reach a peaceful settlement with the ANC. "Some people, specifically in the military, but in the police as well, deep down believed we had to fight it out in some way or another," he recalled. "We at the NIS believed this was the wrong way to go about things. We took the view that a political settlement was the only answer to the problems of this country."[224]

On July 5, 1989, Mandela and Botha met to begin talks. Afterward, Botha expressed his belief that Mandela was interested in pursuing a peaceful settlement.[225] On February 11, 1990, Nelson Mandela finally walked out of prison a free man.

Authorities feared a national uprising similar to what occurred when the Ayatollah Khomeini returned to Iran from exile in 1979 and had declared himself head of a new revolutionary government. Mandela avoided that type of scene, arriving at a public appearance hours late and refraining from delivering a rabble-rousing address. The carefully calculated behavior and subdued demeanor were designed specifically to allay fears among whites that they would be treated as they had treated blacks in the years of segregation and oppression.

Mandela and Botha's successor, F.W. de Klerk, eventually hammered out a political solution that established a government characterized by free elections and majority rule. They shared a Nobel Peace Prize in 1993 for their work in ending apartheid without a violent civil war, achieving the seemingly impossible by creating a state under the principle of "one person, one vote."

---

223 Ibid, 36.
224 Ibid, 50.
225 Ibid, 59.

But doubts still lingered. Decades of tension on both sides were difficult to brush away in a matter of months or even years. Whites were afraid blacks would seize their land. Some groups pushed for the creation of an independent, self-ruling Boer state. More radical black groups instilled fear in whites with their proposed solution, "one settler, one bullet." Mandela, however, the consummate politician and unwavering optimist, started a campaign that would win the loyalty of both blacks and whites.

It began with one of the lessons he learned in prison: white South Africa's passion for the thoroughly tough, physical sport of rugby. The challenge, however, was that most blacks knew nothing about rugby and hated the game as a symbol of the despicable practice of apartheid. Most had made up their minds that they would never have an interest in rugby, now or ever. To them, it was a game played by apartheid's self-proclaimed master race, the Afrikaners.[226]

The South African team known as the Springboks provided more than an occasional diversion. To the whites, it was a religious experience. One of the most critical pressures applied by the international community upon South Africa to end apartheid was a world boycott of the country's rugby team. The team was not allowed to participate in the first two World Cup competitions in 1987 and 1991, a terrible blow to South Africa's prestige. The ANC and international rugby officials eventually agreed to allow the South African team to compete in world competition provided that whites did not use the event to promote apartheid symbols. In 1993, that agreement was broadened to not only allow South Africa to participate in the World Cup games, but also to host the event.

Then, just days after the announcement, Chris Hani, the greatest hero outside of Mandela to apartheid opponents, was assassinated by a member of the white resistance movement. TV images on April 10, 1993, of Hani lying in a pool of blood inflamed the country as no other event had done. These activities brought South Africa as close to civil war as it would ever experience. Mandela, though at the time not a formally elected leader, still served as a de facto head of South Africa's blacks. Mandela went on radio and TV to ask his enraged constituency for restraint: "I appeal, with all the authority at my command, to all our

---

[226] Ibid, 10 − 11.

people to remain calm and honor the memory of Chris Hani by remaining a disciplined force for peace."[227]

Mandela turned the tide. Blacks held mass rallies to express their grief, but the tone was peaceful. South African Archbishop Desmond Tutu, also a 1984 Nobel Peace Prize winner, credited Mandela with averting disaster: "It was one of the most devastating moments and the anger was palpable. Had Nelson not gone on television and radio the way he did. . . our country would have gone up in flames."[228]

In April 1994, Mandela's ANC won 62 percent of the vote in the nation's first multiracial election, and he became South Africa's first black president in May. He then returned to his strategy of using rugby to unite the diverse factions in South Africa. It led to a theme that was a variation of the well-known motto "one person, one vote": One Team, One Country. He then set about to make that theme a reality.

He got help from the Springboks, who agreed to sing both the black and the white national anthems at one of their rugby games. Just as important — and impressive — they were going to do it in the language of the Xhosa people. Morne du Plessis, a former team captain of the Springboks, was named manager of the team. Du Plessis had been responsible for suggesting the team learn the black half of the national anthem. He felt that spectators seeing the team sing only the white national anthem would send the wrong message to South Africa and the world. Mandela helped the cause by wearing a green Springbok cap presented to him by the team. And the day the team won the Rugby World Cup by defeating New Zealand, he wore a team shirt with the team captain's No. 6 on the back.

There was celebration in the streets as blacks and whites recognized their country had reached a significant milestone.

> The inevitable patriotic hysteria in the South African papers next morning, the sense that the country had changed forever, was summarized in the eight-column front-page headline of a newspaper that had the good fortune to be born on that very day, the *Sunday Independent*. "Triumph of the Rainbow Warriors," the newspaper's very first issue screamed. The foreign

---

[227] Ibid, 120.
[228] Ibid.

press got in on the act too, with even the sportswriters almost forgetting to write about the game itself, like the rugby reporter from the Sydney Morning Herald who began his story, "South Africa emphatically became 'one team, one country' yesterday as the rainbow nation went into raptures."[229]

South Africa had regained its stature in the world. Arrie Rossouw, an Afrikaner journalist, expressed the feelings of South African whites about the improvement in the country's image in the eyes of the world. "We were no longer the baddies anymore," he said. "Not only did we win, the world actually wanted us to win. Do you realize what that meant to us? What joy? What enormous relief?"[230]

Mandela served one five-year term as president of South Africa and retired a few weeks before turning 80. But he did not exit the world stage. Since then, he has been instrumental in bringing to trial two suspects believed responsible for bombing Pan Am Flight 103 that crashed in Lockerbie, Scotland, on December 21, 1988. Both men, employees of Libya Arab Airlines, were found in Libya, which held them under house arrest, but refused to allow extradition. Mandela successfully negotiated with Libyan leader Muammar al-Gaddafi to turn the suspects over to authorities for trial in The Netherlands under Scottish law. On January 31, 2001, one was convicted by a court of three Scottish judges and sentenced to life in prison. The second was acquitted.

In 2002, Mandela came out of retirement to create a public awareness campaign about the HIV/AIDS crisis in South Africa, where one of nine citizens is infected with the virus. Mandela revealed that a niece and two sons of a nephew were victims of the disease. He named the campaign "46664," which was his prison number during his 27-year sentence. Then in 2007, he celebrated his 89th birthday by announcing the formation of a group of retired world leaders called The Elders.

These senior diplomats use their education, experience and any other pertinent skills to rise above the concerns of nation, race and creed to make the Earth a more peaceful and equitable place to live. Members include Desmond Tutu, former U.S. Presidents Jimmy Carter

---

229 Ibid, 246.
230 Ibid, 247.

and Bill Clinton, former U.N. secretary-general Kofi Annan, former Irish president Mary Robinson, philanthropist Muhammad Yunas, Indian women's rights campaigner Ela Bhatt and Mandela's wife Graca Machel. Mandela, whose health was growing increasingly frail, decided not to play an active role in the group.

Nelson Mandela's life shows that miracles can, indeed, be accomplished through optimism. One of millions of black victims of apartheid, he could have become negative and turned his anger into raw, savage violence. And it does seem unusual that a jailed terrorist would learn restraint and come out of prison to win the Nobel Peace Prize. Mandela, however, found that the best way to overcome an enemy is to embrace him, writing in his 1995 autobiography, *Long Walk to Freedom*, "If you want to make peace with your enemy, you have to work with your enemy. Then he becomes your partner."

Mandela's optimism carried him far. His natural charm won the hearts and minds of nearly everyone he met. There were no tricks involved. Mandela had a genuine interest in, and concern for, everyone. In some ways, his optimism proved self-fulfilling. His belief in the ultimate success of his efforts may have many times created the positive results that followed. Mandela's life stands as an example to the world: always believe that you can make a difference for the better, and more times than not you will.

# AMELIA EARHART

Radiomen on the U.S. Coast Guard cutter *Itasca* received the last voice radio transmission from American aviation pioneer and explorer Amelia Earhart on July 2, 1937. It was a brief and cryptic message:

"KHAQQ calling *Itasca*. We must be on you but cannot see you. . . gas is running low. . . ." The *Itasca* received the message about 7:30 p.m. Greenwich Mean Time.

The 250-foot Lakes class vessel had been stationed off Howland Island in the Pacific, approximately 1,600 miles southwest of Honolulu, ready for such an emergency. Their mission was to provide air navigation and radio links with Earhart as she completed the last phase of her much publicized 1937 around-the-world flight.

Earhart and navigator Fred Noonan were attempting to reach Howland Island for refueling, but apparently unable to find an island of only 400 dry acres in the vast open waters of the Pacific. At 8:14 p.m. GMT, the ship's crew received one last voice message from Earhart:

"We are in a line position of 157'- 337. Will report on 6210 kilocycles. Wait, listen on 6210 kilocycles. We are running North and South."

The crew of the *Itasca* continued to broadcast on all frequencies until 9:30 p.m. GMT but finally concluded that Earhart's plane had gone down. Despite an intensive two-week search, Amelia was lost forever.

Despite her tragic end, Earhart lived every day of her life as an unending adventure, tackling challenges of space and time with an unflagging optimism and joy for living.

It has been over 80 years since Amelia Earhart rose to fame as "Lady Lindy" — the female face of aviation. Despite a tempestuous childhood and years of yearning to find her place in the world, once Earhart discovered her passion for flight, she became a permanent fixture in the field of aviation. She opened doors for women and blazed her own trail, in the process demonstrating the endless possibilities that aviation could bring to the world. Earhart's countless achievements are a reflection of her can-do attitude and general approach to life — an unrelenting persistence to achieve her goals and a curious, yet wildly independent streak that provided her with the courage to face adversity head on.

Amelia Mary Earhart was born in Atchison, Kansas, on July 24, 1897, to Amy and Edwin Earhart. Her mother was the daughter of Amelia Otis and Judge Alfred Otis, a prominent and wealthy family. Her father was the son of an Evangelical Lutheran missionary who worked his way through college by shining shoes, tending furnaces and tutoring his classmates. With his background, Edwin Earhart did not meet the standards of Amy's parents, who viewed him as an unsuitable match for their daughter. Judge Otis did not give his blessing to the marriage of Edwin and Amy for five years, the amount of time it took for Edwin to earn a salary of at least $50 a month to properly support the judge's daughter.[231] Amelia's birth in 1897 was followed two and a half years later by the arrival of a younger sister, Muriel. The girls spent much of their time in Atchison with their maternal grandparents.[232]

Young Amelia was greatly influenced by the traditional and conservative values of her grandparents due to the summers and long stretches of time she spent with them.[233] But rather than adopting this way of thinking, she fled from many of the conservative ideologies of the time that taught that a woman should cling to her domestic role as a wife and mother. It was a role from which she would flee throughout her adult years. Her mother Amy likely played a part in this as well. She did not believe in molding her children into "nice little girls," and Amelia and Muriel spent hours climbing trees, hunting rats with a rifle, and in general, playing rough for little girls of the era.[234]

The Earhart family was often under great stress because of the fluctuation in Edwin's salary, his growing problems with alcohol, and the regular moves the family had to make. (On lecture tours following her successful Trans-Atlantic flight in 1928, Earhart lightly brushed off comments from attendees when they claimed to be from her hometown. "Which one?" she often replied.) As described by biographer Jean Backus, Amelia and Muriel were often shuttled from genteel poverty to indulgent wealth and then back to poverty again.[235]

---

[231] Jean Backus, *Letters from Amelia: An Intimate Portrait of Amelia Earhart,* (Boston: Beacon Press, 1982), 13.
[232] Jan Parr, *Amelia Earhart: First Lady of Flight,* (London: Franklin Watts, 1997), 12.
[233] Backus, Ibid, 13.
[234] Parr, Ibid, 15.
[235] Backus, Ibid, 15.

Earhart was in her early teens when her father's alcohol problems could no longer be ignored. Amy had determined that the resulting anxieties — Edwin's drinking put his job in jeopardy and created additional financial woes for the family[236] — and the constant relocations were not healthy for Amelia and Muriel. So she and the girls moved to Chicago to live with some family friends.[237]

Earhart's independent streak was highlighted after she began high school in Hyde Park, on the south side of Chicago. As noted by biographer Jan Parr, she often took up unpopular causes in high school, isolating her from other classmates. She was described in her high school yearbook as "the girl in brown who walks alone." At one time she lobbied to have an ineffective teacher removed from the school, believing the teacher was on the payroll simply because of connections within the city government. Earhart's accusation was a bold move for anyone to make, especially a teenager with no friends to back her up in a new school. The teacher was not removed; however, Amelia received permission to spend that class time in the library reading on her own.[238]

Following high school, Earhart attended a prep school in Philadelphia and intended to transfer to Bryn Mawr College. Parr also noted that during this time, she kept newspaper clippings about women who were successful in male-dominated career fields. A handwritten note was found next to an article in her scrapbook that detailed legislation to remove discrimination against women in regard to property rights and grant rights for inheritance. The note read, "This method is not sound. Women will gain economic justice by providing for themselves in all lines of endeavor, not by having laws passed for them."[239] This comment made early in life demonstrates Earhart's passion, persistence and optimism that women could achieve the same success as men, and established her belief in the equality of women in all sectors of society.

During Christmas break in 1917, Earhart visited her sister Muriel in Toronto. Up until this point, she had little exposure to the realities and pain of World War I. As noted by biographer Backus, Earhart described what she saw in Toronto as "men without arms and legs, men who were

---

[236] Mary S. Lovell, *The Sound of Wings: The Life of Amelia Earhart,* (New York: St. Martin's Griffin, reprint edition 2009).
[237] Parr, Ibid, 20.
[238] Ibid.
[239] Ibid, 23-24.

paralyzed and men who were blind." She returned to school for a brief period, but made her way back to Toronto to volunteer as a nurse, feeling that "I can't bear the thought of going back to school and being useless." Her strong and independent personality did not allow her to shy away from difficult situations. She felt a strong sense of duty and remained in Toronto with her sister, serving as a nurse until Armistice Day.[240]

Earhart returned to the States and went on to continue her education at Columbia University in New York as a pre-medical student. While in school at the age of 22, she demonstrated her resistance to conservative and traditional values — or, perhaps better stated, her commitment to a life free of boundaries or restrictions. A letter to her mother, who had left for California to work on her marriage with Edwin, is telling. In it, Earhart makes an effort to relieve some of her mother's anxieties regarding her take on religion:

> Don't think for an instant I would ever become an atheist or even doubter nor lose faith in the [Episcopalian] church's teachings as a whole. That is impossible. But you must admit there is a great deal radically wrong in methods and teachings and results today. Probably no more than yesterday, but the present stands up and waves its paws at me and I see — can't help it. It is not the clergy nor the church itself nor the people that are narrow, but the outside pressure that squeezes them into a routine. . .[241]

In childhood as well as adulthood — and the somewhere in between where Earhart was caught — she resisted any restrictions that were placed upon her. She was independent, free-spirited, and did not hesitate to call into question the conventional wisdom and beliefs to which many clung so tightly. Earhart simply did not accept social norms and expectations; she blazed her own path, avoiding the "outside pressure" that would squeeze her into "a routine."

At 23, Earhart moved to California after her parents asked her to come live with them. Edwin had finally found a secure job, and he and

---

[240] Backus, Ibid, 47.
[241] Ibid, 51.

Amy were working to keep their marriage together. True to her nature and willing to assist where possible, Earhart told her sister Muriel before leaving, "I'll see what I can do to keep Mother and Dad together, Pidge, but after that I'm going to come back here and live my own life."[242] At this point, she had no career direction. But her courageous and independent nature kept her continuously on the move, always searching for purpose in her life.

While in California, Earhart was introduced to flying during an air show on Long Beach with her father. She requested flying lessons and took her first flight the following day in a Los Angeles suburb. Edwin paid the $10 fee for his daughter to be a passenger. She later wrote, "As soon as we left the ground, I knew I myself had to fly."[243] Within a few days, she was signed up for 12 hours of lessons for a hefty $500 fee.[244] When her parents could not help with the money, she began working odd jobs to raise the funds.[245]

She selected as her first flying instructor Neta Snook, who enthralled Earhart with her ability to take on the field of aviation and to dress and talk like a man. While Amelia and Neta became fast friends, the instructor discouraged the student from pursuing flying as a career. She didn't believe Earhart's piloting skills were adequate, and that she was distracted and a little careless. But Earhart persisted and went on to purchase her first plane before her 25th birthday. She scraped together the money between her odd jobs and loans from her sister and mother and bought a Kinner Airster that she called *Canary*.[246] Earhart continued lessons with Neta and, eventually, with an experienced pilot who had trained pilots in World War I. Finally, she made her first solo flight, which did not go as smoothly as planned. She took the plane in too high after a shock absorber broke on takeoff and suffered a rough landing.[247] But she wasn't discouraged, and with characteristic optimism and determination stayed the course on her journey in the field of aviation. Over the next few years, Earhart continued to work to pay for the fuel for her *Canary*. She invited her father and sister to an air show

---

[242] Parr, Ibid, 28.
[243] Ibid, 29.
[244] Lovell, Ibid.
[245] Brenda Haugen, *Amelia Earhart: Legendary Aviator*, (Mankato, Minn.: Compass Point Books, Capstone Publishers, 2007), 37.
[246] Lovell, Ibid.
[247] Parr, Ibid, 34.

in Los Angles, where they watched as Amelia broke her first of many aviation records: the highest altitude reached by a female aviator, 14,000 feet.[248]

In 1924, the tumultuous relationship of Amelia's parents ended as they filed for divorce. Amelia, Muriel and Amy decided to move to the East Coast. Earhart sold the *Canary* and bought a little yellow car to make the then-unusual cross-country drive from Los Angeles to Massachusetts.[249] Now back on the East Coast, Earhart returned to school briefly at Columbia University. While she excelled in academics, she demonstrated little direction when it came to continuing her formal education. Flying was her passion. With the family in need of additional financial support, she left Columbia and accepted a position at Denison House, which provided support to immigrant families throughout Boston. Earhart thrived in this atmosphere. Eventually, her position became fulltime, and she moved into Denison House to continue her work[250] — though her passion for flying was unabated.

Marriage was another social norm that Earhart made a concerted effort to avoid. While living with her parents in California, she was introduced to Sam Chapman, a well-educated chemical engineer. The two enjoyed many of the same activities, including attending illegal meetings of a Socialist group called the Industrial Workers of the World. Later, when Earhart moved to Boston with her mother and sister, Sam followed her.[251] Biographer Parr noted that Chapman was, in Earhart's opinion, old-fashioned in his belief that a husband should support his wife and children. Chapman even went so far as to offer to take any job Earhart wanted him to have, because he thought his long work hours contributed to her resistance to marriage.

This offer only served to upset Earhart, who told her sister, "I don't want to tell Sam what he should do. He ought to know what makes him happiest, and then do it, no matter what other people say. I know what I want to do, and I expect to do it, married or single."[252] What she wanted to do was fly, and Earhart would not allow any relationship to hinder her ability to do so — which included turning down his repeated requests for her hand in marriage. Her acceptance of the fulltime

[248] Haugen, 40.
[249] Ibid, 39-40.
[250] Parr, Ibid, 37-38.
[251] Lovell, Ibid.
[252] Parr, Ibid, 38.

position at Denison House and her subsequent move into the home was a major blow to her relationship with Chapman, and their courtship eventually ended after Earhart's successful Trans-Atlantic flight in 1928.[253]

Her love of flying strengthened while in Boston. She won recognition and, according to the *Boston Globe,* was "one of the best women pilots in the United States."[254] During this time, Earhart worked hard to not only log as many hours as possible in her plane, but also to promote the field of aviation. According to biographers Elgen and Marie Long, by 1927, Earhart had logged nearly 500 solo flying hours, a notable achievement for any pilot.[255] She wrote columns in local newspapers and set the stage for creating an organization devoted to female fliers.[256] Her dedication to aviation was further demonstrated by her services as a sales representative for Kinner airplanes and her financial investment in the Dennison Airport,[257] from which she took the first official flight in 1927.[258]

In May 1927, aviation and the possibilities it provided attracted a great deal of publicity. Charles Lindbergh made the first solo flight from Long Island, New York, to Paris in 33 hours and 30 minutes. The 25-year-old pilot became an American hero, made headlines and emerged as an instant celebrity at home and abroad.[259] He also brought aviation to the forefront of the world's attention.

Following Lindbergh's flight, Earhart received a phone call that would arguably alter the course of the rest of her life and almost certainly change aviation and women's roles in that field. The caller invited her to do some flying that could be dangerous. Intrigued, Earhart sought to learn more. She discovered it was to be the first

253 Parr, Ibid, 40.
254 AmeliaEarhart.net: Celebrating the Greatest Woman Pilot in History, www.ameliaearhart.net/biography/, accessed April 26, 2010.
255 Elgen M. Long and Marie K. Long, *Amelia Earhart: The Mystery Solved,* (New York: Simon & Schuster, 2000), 38.
256 Blythe Randolph,. *Amelia Earhart: Impact Biographies Series.* (London: Franklin Watts, 1987).
257 Doris L. Rich, *Amelia Earhart: A Biography,* (Washington and London: Smithsonian Institution Press, 1989),43.
258 Stephanie Chaisson, "Squantum Has a Hold on Its Residents," (Quincy, Mass.: *The Patriot Ledger,* July 12, 2007), www.patriotledger.com/lifestyle/house_and_home/x1709132033, accessed April 26, 2010.
259 Leonard Mosley, *Lindbergh: A Biography,* (New York: Doubleday, 1976).

Trans-Atlantic flight successfully completed by a female aviator. It was sponsored by Amy Phipps Guest, the daughter of American industrialist Henry Phipps and wife of Britain's former Secretary of State for Air. Guest was seeking a female pilot to take on the expedition with a male crew. She had purchased a Fokker F7 airplane that she named the *Friendship* and had made plans herself to become the first woman to fly the Atlantic. But her family had persuaded her not to try the flight, creating an opportunity for Earhart.[260]

Earhart left for New York for a more in-depth meeting about the flight. Her resemblance to Lindbergh was not lost on anyone, and they viewed her as an intelligent and attractive female pilot — perfect for the famous flight. At this meeting, she was introduced to her future husband, George Palmer Putman, who would serve as publicist for the flight and, consequently, for Earhart. It was a task Putnam took on throughout the remainder of her career.[261]

Earhart had to keep the news of the event from her family to ensure the media did not get wind of the plan prior to takeoff, and she had requested that her onetime suitor Sam Chapman inform her mother and sister as soon as the flight had departed. However, before anyone was able to talk with Muriel and Amy, calls from reporters started to come to the house. A day into the trip, when Earhart landed in Newfoundland, she sent a cable to her mother that said, "Know you will understand why I could not tell you plans of the flight. Don't worry. No matter what happens it will have been worth trying. Love, A." Amy responded, "We are not worrying. Wish I were with you. Good luck and cheerio. Love, Mother."[262] As this cable clearly illustrates, Earhart remained optimistic and upbeat despite the dangers she faced.

Fog held up the *Friendship* for almost two weeks before conditions were safe for flying once again, and the aircraft finally took off from Halifax, Newfoundland, on June 17, 1928. Hours into the last leg of their flight, Earhart and the crew were worried.[263] With only an hour's worth of fuel left, no land was yet in sight. Surrounded by fog, the crew finally spotted land and brought the plane down, unaware of the location. Eventually, they were picked up by a small boat and discovered they had

---

[260] Susan Butler *East to the Dawn: The Life of Amelia Earhart,* (Cambridge, Mass.: Da Capo Press, a member of the Perseus Books Group, 1999), 150.
[261] Parr, Ibid, 40.
[262] Ibid, 43.
[263] Ibid, 44.

arrived in Burry Port, Wales — not far from Southampton, England, their original destination.

Within the brief period between the flight's landing and the crew being transported to the local village, a couple hundred people had gathered to greet the new celebrities. Earhart directed attention to others, including the flight's crew, Bill Stultz and Lou Gordon: "The credit belongs to [the crew] and to the flight's backer as well as to the manufacturers of the plane and motors." Nevertheless, Earhart emerged as an overnight sensation by becoming the first female aviator to cross the Atlantic. The *Friendship* crew spent time in London, where they were guests of honor at receptions, went to parties and were invited to give speeches. After returning to the United States, they took part in parades and events to celebrate their success.[264]

Interestingly, during the famous flight, Earhart did not actively participate in manning the airplane. She kept the logbooks and referred to herself on the trip as a "worthless sack of potatoes."[265] But she was not recognized for her piloting efforts, which she did not demonstrate on this flight. Rather, it was her attempt to become the first female to cross the Atlantic. In letters to her mother and Muriel, Amelia wrote that if she were to "pop off" she hoped they wouldn't be too upset, as it was a great way to go. This example of courage only hinted at the bold steps Amelia took during her day.[266] Shortly after the flight, Amelia wrote her first book, *20 hrs. 40 min.*, with the help of publicist Putman and his secretary while staying at her husband-to-be's home in New York.[267]

Putman's marriage to his first wife Dorothy had been in trouble for some time, and two years after he began representing Earhart the two filed for divorce.[268] Earhart had always stayed away from marriage for fear it would hinder her ability to make her own career decisions. Putman proposed more than a half-dozen times before Earhart accepted. Still fearing the social constraints that marriage could bring and true to her independent nature, she had a letter delivered to Putman before they were married. It read in part:

---

[264] Ibid, 47.
[265] Backus, Ibid, 72.
[266] Ibid, 65.
[267] Long and Long, Ibid, 44.
[268] Parr, 49.

You must know again my reluctancy to marry, my feeling that I shatter thereby chances in work which means so much to me. I feel the move just now as foolish as anything I could do. I know there may be compensations, but I have no heart to look ahead.[269]

While Earhart did indeed enter into the "confines of marriage," she did continue to act independently by keeping her own name, an action remarkable for that era when most wives accepted their husband's last name.[270]

After finishing the book, Putman helped Amelia complete the publicity and lecture appearances arranged for her. During these events she became aware of their potential to help her secure additional funding and sponsorships that would allow more record-setting flights. Encouraged by Putman, she signed on as a spokeswoman for many products, including luggage, women's clothing and sportswear, as well as for Lucky Strike cigarettes — which caused her some image problems.[271] During this time, she also took a position as an associate editor with *Cosmopolitan* magazine, which allowed her to continue to build her brand. Earhart utilized her column in the magazine as a forum to promote acceptance of aviation as a viable means of transportation and to encourage acceptance and inclusion of women in the field.[272]

Earhart's viewpoint on the role aviation could take in the future was arguably visionary and undoubtedly optimistic for her time. She was among the first aviators to promote air travel, becoming involved not only as a representative and advocate, but also financially in a regional shuttle service that would later become TWA. Additionally, she served as vice president for National Airways.[273] Earhart also utilized her time at the lecture podium — speaking to organizations composed mostly of women — to encourage the use of air travel for business purposes.[274] In the 1920s and 1930s, flight was still a relatively new and foreign concept to most of the world. After all, the Wright brothers had just made the

[269] Ibid, 52-53.
[270] Ibid, 54.
[271] Ware, Ibid, 97-98.
[272] C.V. Glines, "'Lady Lindy': The Remarkable Life of Amelia Earhart." *Aviation History*, July 1997.
[273] *Boston and Maine Railroad Employees Magazine*, Volume 8, Number 10, July 1933.
[274] Backus, Ibid, 83.

first successful flight in the early part of the 20<sup>th</sup> century.[275] It was assumed that more men would travel for business if their wives felt comfortable with the notion, a topic that could not be delivered as effectively by anyone other than Earhart.

Earhart and Putman were aware that to continue to ensure that fresh material was available for her speeches and lectures, she would need to continue to make newsworthy and record-setting achievements. That was fine with Earhart, who would have much preferred to be in the air anyway.[276] In 1929 she made her first attempt at competitive air racing at the inaugural Women's Air Derby. She fought to ensure that the race was fair and offered a chance for female pilots to come together. At one point during the negotiations for the derby, it was suggested that a male navigator be required to fly with each female pilot. Earhart responded, "If we can't fly the race and navigate our own course. . . I, for one, won't enter." She finished third in the competition, but later she pronounced that the competition "added considerably to our flying knowledge, and at the same time, served to increase public interest and confidence in women in aviation."[277]

Earhart once wrote, "Women must try to do things as men have tried. When they fail, their failure must be but a challenge to others."[278] Putting words into action, she continued to actively seek additional records to break and maintained a desire to prove herself in the field of aviation. It was 1932 when she decided to fly the Atlantic solo, something that had not been accomplished since Lindbergh had done it five years earlier.[279]

Earhart had many reasons for wanting to make the flight. However, first and foremost was a personal need to prove to herself that, despite being merely a passenger on the 1928 flight that catapulted her to fame, she had the skills to do it on her own. Biographers have also noted that despite Putman's successful efforts to place her in the public spotlight as the best-known female pilot, Earhart needed to prove that she was the

---

[275] James Tobin, *The Wright Brothers and the Great Race for Flight* (New York: Free Press, a division of Simon & Schuster, 2003).
[276] Backus, Ibid.
[277] Ware, Ibid, 82.
[278] Beatrice Gormely, *Amelia Earhart: Young Aviator*, (New York: Aladdin Paperbacks, an imprint of Simon & Schuster Children's Publishing Division, 2000), *270*.
[279] Parr, Ibid, 52.

best woman pilot.[280] She made public statements clarifying that her solo flight would not contribute anything to the field of aviation. "It was clear in my mind that I was undertaking the flight merely for the fun of it," she said. "It was a measure, a self-justification — a proving to me, and to anyone else interested, that a woman with adequate experience could do it."[281]

Five years to the day that Lindbergh had set off on his journey across the Atlantic, Earhart took flight. The obstacles she faced in the air were nearly insurmountable, including a failed altimeter only a few hours into the air, violent storms, ice buildup on her wings and a leaking reserve fuel tank. But on May 21, 1932 — 14 hours and 54 minutes after beginning her journey — she successfully brought the plane down in a pasture near Londonderry in Northern Ireland.[282] She had thrust herself into the international spotlight by flying again across the Atlantic, not as a "sack of potatoes" but as the sole pilot of a single-engine Lockheed Vega.

By the following day, a crew from Paramount News had arrived, along with reporters, photographers and a large crowd that had gathered to greet Earhart. She posed for pictures with her airplane and put on her flying suit to reenact the landing. Congratulatory letters arrived from President Hoover, Charles Lindbergh, the prime minister of Britain and then-Governor Franklin Roosevelt and his wife Eleanor.[283]

Earhart had accomplished what no other female in aviation had thus far been able to do. While the public had seen her as an accomplished aviator previously, the solo flight firmly placed her in an elite class of aviators. Typically, she downplayed the idea that she possessed any special courage, telling a newspaper reporter: "If it took courage I wouldn't have done it... I undertook the flight for my own pleasure and in a sense to justify myself."[284]

Following this success, Earhart returned to the United States to give speeches and lectures, and continued to speak her mind and confront issues that many avoided. For example, at a meeting of the Daughters of

---

[280] Lovell, Ibid.
[281] Amelia Earhart, *The Fun of It: Random Records of My Own Flying and of Women in Aviation* (Chicago: Academy Chicago Publishers, 2006).
[282] Lovell, Ibid.
[283] Gormely, Ibid, 224.
[284] Parr, Ibid, 64.

the American Revolution, she openly criticized the organization for campaigning for a weapons buildup in preparation for another war. She argued that they did not have a right to call for war if they themselves were not willing to serve.[285] These comments, while not well received by the organization, demonstrated Earhart's optimism that women could do anything men could do; at the same time, they underlined an aversion to war that had grown from seeing its effects during her time as a nurse in Canada during World War I.

In late 1934, Earhart began planning another big flight, this time from Hawaii to California. Others had flown from California to Hawaii, but Amelia would be the first to fly from Hawaii to California.[286] Earhart knew that flying over land was one thing— there was always somewhere to land. However, it was much riskier to fly over water. But in January 1935, she became the first person to fly solo across the Pacific Ocean.[287]

Following this flight, she received a letter from President Franklin Roosevelt, who wrote she had "shown even the 'doubting Thomases' that aviation is a science which cannot be limited to men only." Roosevelt also referred to the prospect of trans-ocean air travel, seemingly crediting Earhart with helping to open the door to these possibilities.[288] Clearly, Roosevelt recognized her courage and optimistic approach toward the potential of aviation and the advances it could bring to society.

At the personal request of the consul general of Mexico, Earhart completed the first solo flight from California to Mexico City, then took a position at Purdue University in Lafayette, Indiana.[289] She had previously met the university president, Dr. Edward C. Elliott, and he had been so impressed with her optimism over career possibilities for young women that he invited her to the school. Earhart signed on as a consultant in the department for the study of careers for women.[290] This led to an increase of freshman women enrolling at the university — 50 percent during her first year there.[291] Biographer Parr noted that Earhart greatly enjoyed her time at the school, where she stayed in a

---

[285] Ibid, 68.
[286] Ibid, 69.
[287] Jane Sutcliffe, *Amelia Earhart: History Maker Bios, 45*.
[288] Lovell, Ibid.
[289] Parr, Ibid, 73.
[290] Lovell, Ibid.
[291] Butler, Ibid, 317.

dormitory and ate meals and visited with the students.[292] During her first lecture, Earhart discussed the nudging of the glass ceiling and cracking open the door to opportunities for women: "Things are changing so rapidly. . . the opportunity for employment upon graduation from college is better than it has been, and promises to expand even more."[293]

While staying busy at Purdue and with her lecture tours, Earhart remained keenly aware that there were few aviation records left to break. One feat that had not been attempted was round-the-world flight at the equator. Earhart set her sights on being the first to do it, realizing that her future would be secure if she accomplished this goal.[294] While Earhart did have her supporters in taking on this treacherous flight, including Putman, many tried to talk her out of taking the risk. She responded:

> I've wanted to do this flight for a long time. . . I've worked hard and I deserve one fling during my lifetime. If I should pop off, it should be doing the thing I've always wanted most to do. . . The Man with the little black book has a date marked down for all us — when our work here is finished.[295]

In the past, Earhart's flights had always been chartered by someone before her; she was just the first person to go alone or the first woman or the first to make the flight in a shorter period of time. Earhart wanted to take on this challenge and blaze her own trail.[296] Her unrelenting persistence when it came to facing and achieving her goals was on full display. Without an optimistic belief that it could be done, the effort would have never gained traction.

Earhart's file showed that she gave 136 speeches and lectures in 1936, keeping her busy traveling and on the road.[297] Meanwhile, Putman helped in flight preparations. In addition to hiring necessary staff and consulting on plans, he worked with President Roosevelt to ensure that

---

[292] Parr, Ibid, 73.
[293] Butler, Ibid, 317.
[294] Parr, Ibid, 75.
[295] Haugen, Ibid, 87.
[296] Parr, Ibid, 75.
[297] Lovell, Ibid.

Earhart received assistance from the State Department in gaining clearances from the many countries she was to fly over. Their friendship with the Roosevelts allowed Earhart and Putman to gain the clearances — which typically take weeks or months — in a matter of days.[298] The preparations also included the need for a bigger plane. Amelia settled on the Lockheed Electra, a twin-engine aircraft that could fly up to 4,000 miles without refueling.[299] She also had to learn how to fly the Electra, whose engines and controls were much more sophisticated than she was accustomed to using.[300]

Despite many roadblocks, Earhart persisted. As biographer Lovell writes, she felt that if she abandoned the attempt, she would be remembered as the woman who once tried to fly around the world and failed. She feared that her achievements would simply be forgotten. Lovell says that Earhart's character, a determination that amounted to stubbornness and pride in her reputation, left her with the notion that she had to make this attempt.[301]

Prior to leaving, Earhart realized the risk she was taking and assumed full responsibility for what might happen, telling Putman before she left, "I know that if I fail or if I am lost you will be blamed for allowing me to leave on this trip; the backers of the flight will be blamed and everyone connected with it. But it's my responsibility and mine alone."[302]

On February 12, 1937, she held a press conference in New York City to announce the flight and on March 18, 1937, newspaper headlines read, "Miss Earhart Off on World Flight." Along with navigators Harry Manning and Fred Noonan and the flight's technical advisor, Paul Mantz, Earhart took off, flying east to west to begin the journey.[303]

The flight did not always go as smoothly as planned, but Earhart was finally nearing the end. She and Noonan, who remained for the final leg of the journey to assist her in navigation, took off from New Guinea for Howland Island, a trip that was expected to take 18 hours. This portion of the journey was considered the most difficult because finding

---

[298] Parr, Ibid, 76.
[299] Sutcliffe, Ibid.
[300] Lovell, Ibid.
[301] Lovell, Ibid.
[302] Ibid.
[303] Ware, Ibid, 216.

Howland Island was like looking for a needle in a haystack.[304] The U.S. Department of the Interior had built a runway on the island specifically to provide a location for refueling during the flight. From Howland Island, Earhart and Noonan were to fly to Hawaii and then from Hawaii to California — completing their journey.[305]

They never arrived, and their disappearance serves as the basis for one of the most intriguing mysteries of the 20th century. Within an hour after final radio contact with Earhart, a search party was sent out to an area where—based upon fuel consumption estimates—the plane most likely would have run out of gas. The initial $4 million search lasted for a full week with no sign of Earhart, Noonan or the plane. Additional searches continued for weeks and months, covering a large expanse of the Pacific Ocean. Altogether, it was the most extensive sea search in U.S. history.[306]

Her disappearance was front-page news—huge, bold headlines screamed, "Amelia Lost!" It is assumed that the plane went down in the Pacific, but no evidence was ever found to support that conclusion. Speculation about what really happened continues to this day. In *Still Missing: Amelia Earhart and the Search for Modern Feminism*, Susan Ware argues that the unresolved circumstances of the disappearance have kept Earhart in the public spotlight far longer than if she had returned home safely.[307]

Earhart, an iconic American woman with the courage to face adversity every step of the way, once said, "If we don't burn up, I want to try again." She embodied the confidence and strength of today's successful woman[308] — but without the opportunities of today's society. Her optimistic approach to life and its possibilities enabled Amelia Earhart to soar to heights that were unexpected by anyone other than herself.

---

[304] Ware, Ibid, 222.
[305] Parr, Ibid, 85.
[306] Ware, Ibid, 223.
[307] Ibid, 228.
[308] Lovell, Ibid.

# JOHN MCCAIN

On October 26, 1967, a 31-year-old U.S. Navy pilot was flying his 23rd combat mission over Hanoi when a North Vietnamese anti-aircraft missile blew a wing off his A-4E Skyhawk as he completed a bombing run.

The aircraft went into a violent, uncontrollable spin, but the young Navy flier successfully ejected. The force of the ejection, however, broke both arms and his right leg and knocked him unconscious. As the wounded pilot floated down, he regained consciousness, and his parachute dropped him into a small lake in a park in Hanoi.

The dashing lieutenant commander almost drowned. His painful broken limbs prevented him from swimming or even treading water. The more than 50 pounds of equipment he carried began pulling him under. He finally activated a toggle switch with his teeth that inflated his life jacket. He bobbed to the surface for a gulp of life-saving air.

A group of North Vietnamese men went into the water and pulled him out of the lake, and an angry mob quickly assembled. They ripped off his clothes, beat him severely, crushed his shoulder with the butt of a rifle and bayoneted him in his left foot and groin. A broken bone protruded from his shattered right knee.

His captors took him to Hoa Lo, a prisoner of war camp American POWs dubbed, "The Hanoi Hilton." Thus began a 5½ -year ordeal that, inconceivably, would only get worse. The flier would be imprisoned with inadequate medical care and suffer severe beatings and psychological torture.

He would persevere, however, and survive. He would become a member of the U.S. House of Representatives, a U.S. Senator and his party's 2008 nominee for president. He is the senior U.S. Senator from Arizona, the Honorable John S. McCain III.

McCain's story is by now familiar to most Americans. It is one of bravery and optimism, survival and triumph, inspiration and respect — qualities that were not lost on his captors. It has been reported that his wartime jailer even admitted in June 2008 that if he had the opportunity, he would vote for the Senator "because of McCain's willingness to forgive and look to the future."[309] The jailer, Tran Trong Duyet, reportedly said, "If I were an American voter, I would vote for John McCain. He's very loyal to the U.S. military, to his beliefs, and to his country. In all of our debates, he never admitted that the war was a mistake." Duyet claims the two were friends, and that he spent off-duty time conversing with McCain.[310]

At a fund-raising luncheon in California during his bid for the presidency, McCain's wife Cindy praised his ability to move beyond the tortures he endured at the "Hanoi Hilton." "He reconciled," she said. "He became a part of the process that enabled Vietnam to have a normal relationship with the United States, the normalization, as you all remember. In my opinion, my husband embodies the essence of what America is all about. The essence of hope, freedom, forgiveness, understanding and world leadership. It takes a strong person to do what he did. I'm very proud of my husband."[311] I too am proud of John McCain. He is a friend and one of my greatest heroes.

John McCain grew from military roots. Both his father and grandfather were four-star admirals. Adm. John S. McCain Jr. was commander in chief of all U.S. forces in the Pacific during the Vietnam War. His grandfather rose to the rank of four-star admiral during World War II. At the end of the war, John McCain Jr. witnessed the Japanese surrender aboard the U.S.S. *Missouri*. McCain's great uncle also served as an Army general during World War I.[312]

This distinguished military lineage also affected McCain when he was in enemy hands. Initially, his broken bones and other injuries from the crash were left untreated as a means of torture. After withstanding all the pain he could, McCain told his captors he would give them

309 Ambreen Ali, "Hanoi Captor Endorses McCain, Denies Torture: Duyet calls ex-POW a friend," Newser.com, June 28, 2008, www.newser.com/story/31144/hanoi-captor-endorses-mccain-denies-torture.html, accessed November 12, 2009.
310 Ibid.
311 Michael Cooper, "McCain Talks about POW Experiences," The Caucus: The Politics and Government Blog of The *Times*, The New York *Times*, July 28, 2008, thecaucus.blogs.nytimes.com/2008/07/28/mccain-talks-about-pow-experiences/ , accessed November 12, 2009.
312 John S. McCain III. "John McCain, Prisoner of War: A First-Person Account," U.S. *News & World Report*, originally published May 14, 1973, posted online January 28, 2008, accessed online November 3, 2009 www.usnews.com/articles/news/2008/01/28/john-mccain-prisoner-of-war-a-first-person-account.html.

information if they took him to the hospital. A so-called doctor took John's pulse and announced it was "too late."[313] They expected him to die of his injuries.

McCain passed out from the agonizing pain, but one of his captors came rushing in to announce they had learned, "Your father is a big admiral; now we take you to the hospital."[314] His captors administered blood and intravenous solutions, which enabled McCain to regain some of his lucidity. After learning of his famous father, they were particularly interested in getting a propaganda statement from McCain. They wanted him to admit to his "crimes" and to state for television audiences that the Vietnamese had treated him well. In return, they offered early release.

U.S. military regulations, however, require that prisoners of war be released in the order in which they are captured. McCain was adamant about honoring that code. He would not shortchange a fellow soldier for his own freedom. Because he would not cooperate, he was held in solitary confinement for much of his captivity.

That experience and McCain's steadfastness to a principle greater than his own interests helped shape his vision. In his memoir, *Faith of Our Fathers,* McCain expressed a core value that has guided him throughout his public life: "Glory belongs to the act of being constant to something greater than yourself, to a cause, to your principles, to the people on whom you rely, and who rely on you in return." It is this resilient and courageous attitude that has taken McCain through adversity in his personal, professional and political life, and made him a shining example of perseverance borne from optimism.

McCain was born in the Panama Canal Zone, where his father was stationed. They were constantly on the move as his father, an active duty admiral in the Navy, was transferred from one military assignment to another. McCain's courage and optimism served him well, often taking away the sting of being the new kid in school. In 1951 when he attended Episcopal High School, an exclusive boarding school in Alexandria, Virginia, McCain finally felt as if he had found a home, a thought he expressed in 2008 when he returned to his alma mater to hold a town hall meeting:

---

[313] Ibid.
[314] Ibid.

If there is any reason for my success in life, it is because of what I learned at The High School, much of it through the Honor Code. I learned that character is what you are in the dark. . . I have been in the dark, not just in prison but also in my public life, and during those times and throughout my life, the principles of the Honor Code are the compass that I've tried to follow.[315]

Things were not always smooth sailing for the occasionally belligerent student, however. His quick temper and fists earned him the nickname "McNasty" among his fellow classmates. An entry included in McCain's senior yearbook referred to him as a "punk" and noted that he had a magnetic personality, which sometimes attracts and sometimes repels:

It was three fateful years ago that the "Punk" first crossed the threshold of The High School. In this time he has become infamous as one of our top-flight wrestlers, lettering for two seasons. His magnetic personality has won for him many life-long friends. But, as magnets must also repel, some have found him hard to get along with. John is remarkable for the amount of gray hair he has; this may come from his cramming for Annapolis or from his nocturnal perambulations. The Naval Academy is his future abode—we hope he will prosper there.[316]

Despite the ups and downs of his youth, McCain's optimism led him to follow in the footsteps of his father and grandfather by enrolling in the U.S. Naval Academy. Other young men of similar temper might well have chafed under the military regimentation and discipline that would

315 *Episcopal High School News*, " 'Episcopal Offered Me a Home' McCain Praises Honor Code, Recalls Beloved Teacher," April 1, 2008. www.episcopalhighschool.org/news/detail.aspx?pageaction=ViewSinglePublic& LinkID=10&ModuleID=11&NEWSPID=5, accessed November 6, 2009.
316 Episcopal High School John S. McCain III Web page. www.episcopalhighschool.org/about_ehs/media_inquiries/john_mccain_54/in dex.aspx, accessed November 6, 2009.

have to be endured. But McCain was optimistic that he would be able to adapt to the demands of Annapolis and the life of service.

However, McCain also found it difficult to keep out of trouble. He had the dubious achievement of being a leader in gathering demerits for minor offenses, such as messy quarters or shoes that needed shining. When he graduated from Annapolis, he was fifth from the bottom in a class of nearly 900, mainly because of his accumulated demerits. Despite his less-than-exemplary record, McCain optimistically applied for flight school. To the surprise of many, he was accepted.

As might be expected, McCain continued to follow the beat of his own drummer. "Graduation transformed neither his style nor his low tolerance for authority," author Robert Timberg writes in *John McCain: An American Odyssey*:

> One night he was playing shuffleboard at the Officer's Club. His nondescript outfit included cowboy boots and a chewed-up crewneck sweater. A cigarette dangled from his lips as an irate commander stormed over. "Ensign McCain, your appearance is a disgrace," said the officer, four grades his senior. "What do you think your grandfather would say?" Squinting through the smoke, McCain replied, "Frankly Commander, I don't think he'd give a rat's ass."[317]

McCain drove a fast Corvette and dated fast women, such as an exotic dancer called the "Flame of Florida."[318] He eventually married Carol Shepp, a beautiful model, and adopted Shepp's two sons. The married couple also had a daughter of their own. But while he was in Vietnam, McCain's wife suffered serious injuries in an automobile accident. McCain did not learn about her accident until he returned from Vietnam, also crippled by his war injuries. At this point, the couple's marriage began to dissolve under the weight of McCain's activities and his wife's disabilities.

---

[317] Robert Timburg, *John McCain: An American Odyssey* (New York: Touchstone, 1995), 66.
[318] Elizabeth Holmes, "McCain and Flame of Florida" Washington Wire: Political Insight and Analysis From The Wall Street Journal's Capital Bureau, blogs.wsj.com/washwire/2008/04/03/mccain-and-flame-of-florida/, April 3, 2008, accessed November 6, 2009.

Then he met a young teacher named Cindy Hensley, whose father was a multi-millionaire owner of a beer distributorship in Arizona. McCain began dating Hensley and asked Carol for a divorce. This was both a public and private embarrassment for McCain. In an interview on CNN with evangelist Rick Warren, McCain was asked about his "greatest moral failure." McCain responded that it was the demise of his first marriage. McCain and Cindy Hensley were married in May 1980 after his divorce was finalized. His children with Shepp—daughter, Sidney, and sons, Doug and Andy from Carol Shepp's first marriage, whom McCain adopted—did not approve of the relationship and did not attend the wedding. Feelings were raw, and it would be several years before the children would interact with McCain.[319] Carol, now retired in Virginia, has never met Cindy.

Yet despite the potential for a life-long, acrimonious relationship between the two, John and Carol apparently have reconciled themselves to what happened and have moved on. In McCain's first political race, an opponent interviewed Carol, looking for negative subject matter to use against him. "I told [the opponent] I believe in John McCain," she said. "He's a good person. I wish him every bit of success."[320]

McCain's military life had been undergoing change as well. In 1977 he began serving the Navy in a different way, becoming a liaison to the U.S. Senate. One of his first actions was to shoot down the opposition by then-President Jimmy Carter to the building of a new-generation aircraft carrier dubbed a "supercarrier." McCain, dedicated to doing things in the best interest of the service, pushed for congressional opposition to Carter.[321] In the policy fight that followed, McCain drew upon the strength of his optimism, displaying one of his defining qualities: never giving up when doing what he believes is right. Guided by this principle, he worked behind the scenes to win over influential senators against the wishes of the Carter White House and even the Navy.

---

[319] Paul Farhi, "The Separate Peace of John And Carol: In the Demise of His First Marriage, John McCain's Life Seems to Have Found a New Path," The Washington *Post,* October 6, 2008, marriage.about.com/gi/o.htm?zi= 1/XJ&zTi=1&sdn=marriage&cdn=people&tm=523&gps=311_313_1020_561&f=10&su=p284.9.336.ip_&tt=11&bt=0&bts=0&zu=http%3A//www.washingtonpost.com/wp-dyn/content/article/2008/10/05/AR2008100502589.html , accessed November 9, 2009.

[320] Ibid, 5.

[321] Robert Timberg, *The Nightengale's Song,* (New York: Touchstone, 1996), 269.

During his tenure as liaison with the Senate, McCain realized he had a strong interest in public service. This, combined with the realization that he might never be promoted in the military, led McCain to retire from the Navy. He moved to Arizona to run for Congress, earning the derogatory label of "carpetbagger." But McCain's energy and optimism helped him overcome the name-calling and eventually win two terms in Congress. He then successfully ran for the U.S. Senate seat left vacant by the retirement of conservative icon Barry Goldwater in 1987 and has served in the Senate since. He is seeking a fifth term in 2010.[322]

McCain's honesty with voters has enabled him to beat back serious political challenges that would have derailed the careers of lesser candidates — and lesser men. In the late 1980s, he was involved in a public scandal referred to as the "Keating Five." This involved five senators, including McCain, who were accused of ethics violations by improperly intervening in 1987 on behalf of Charles H. Keating, Jr., chairman of the Lincoln Savings and Loan Association. The S&L was the target of a regulatory investigation by the Federal Home Loan Bank Board, which eventually abandoned further action. Lincoln S&L finally failed, wiping out the savings of its depositors and costing taxpayers more than $3 billion. One of the five senators was censured and McCain and three others were reprimanded for using poor judgment. Keating was convicted on fraud and racketeering charges, but the convictions were overturned after he served nearly five years in prison.

Many politicians would be devastated by this kind of scandal. McCain, originally greatly affected by his apparent lapse in judgment, assumed the viewpoint of an optimist. He staked his political and personal recovery on the ability of voters to forgive those public figures who are honest and admit they made a mistake. *Time* magazine's Joe Klein recalled an interview with McCain in which the Arizona Senator revealed how badly the experience affected his self-image and morale. Klein wrote:

> I remember this very clearly; it was at the Republican
> Convention in 1996 and it was not out of context—that
> the Keating Five episode was harder, in some ways,

[322] Brian Montopoli, "McCain Will Run For Reelection In 2010," CBS News Blog, November 25, 2008, www.cbsnews.com/blogs/2008/11/25/politics/horserace/ entry4633124.shtml, accessed November 11, 2009.

than being a prisoner of war because his honor had been called into question. He said there were some days that he was so bummed he could barely leave the house. I took these remarks as strong evidence of McCain's candor and humanity—they were the sort of thing few other politicians would have the guts to say . . . [323]

McCain would recover from these events and run for the presidency twice. The first time he ran in 2000, Texas Governor George W. Bush would edge him out in the Republican primaries. Eight years later, he became the party's nominee for President, losing to the Democratic Senator from Illinois, Barack Obama. A pessimist would never have attempted to run for the highest office in the land with the Keating Five scandal hanging around his neck. But McCain — who was later cleared of any wrongdoing by the Senate Ethics Committee — believed in himself and the electorate's willingness to listen to his explanations and judge him accordingly and fairly.

Perhaps McCain's greatest example of optimism can be seen in his family life. By 1988, he and wife Cindy had three children of their own, a daughter and two sons. In 1991, they adopted a daughter from Mother Teresa's orphanage in Bangladesh. McCain's positive outlook on the future of the United States—to say nothing of his faith in his nation—no doubt accounted for his willingness to produce a large family.

McCain's optimism hit a high point in 2008 with his nomination for president. The fact that he chose to run for the nation's most powerful office in 2008 is a testament to this spirit and speaks to his confidence and commitment to remaining in public service. Any Republican candidate following on the heels of President Bush in 2008 was destined to have an uphill struggle. Many political pundits viewed 2008 as a year for Democrats. But McCain took up the challenge. His belief in his ability to attract conservative voters made the election tight throughout the summer. The week after Obama's nomination at the Democratic National Convention August 25 – 28, the Illinois Democrat led McCain by 8 points, 50 to 42 percent, according to Gallup's Daily Tracking Poll.

---

[323] Joe Klein, "The McCain Interview," Swampland: A Blog about Politics, August 28, 2008, Time.com, swampland.blogs.time.com/2008/08/28/ the_mccain_ interview/, accessed November 11, 2009.

However, McCain's great optimism and enthusiasm for America made a tremendous impression on voters during the Republican National Convention September 1 – 4, 2008. This, plus McCain's bold move to select Alaska Gov. Sarah Palin as his running mate, propelled the Republican ticket into the lead. According to a *USA Today*/Gallup poll during September 5 – 7, "likely voters" gave McCain a 10-point lead over Obama, 54 to 44 percent. But the McCain/Palin ticket could not sustain that lead, and poll numbers began to slide in the fall. By October 10, Obama had taken a 10-point lead, 51-41, and went on to win 52.9 percent of the vote on Election Day to McCain's 45.6.

Still driven by his endless optimism, McCain did not seek retirement following the election loss. He returned to the Senate to fight for conservative values.

John McCain continues to play an important role in shaping the America of tomorrow. He can envision the future and possesses the positive, optimistic outlook to believe in our country's integrity and to serve as a role model for the rest of the world. He is a patriot, optimist and leader, and a steward of those traits and values that are uniquely American.

# MOSES

When the Almighty interviewed Moses for the important position of messenger of God's words to the people of Israel, He must have gotten the impression that Moses did not really want the job. His demeanor as described in Exodus was less like actor Charleton Heston's rugged movie portrayal and more like a whining Woody Allen. Moses raised every objection in the book:

- He was not worthy of such an awesome task
- He did not know enough about God
- The people will not listen to him or believe his words
- He claimed he was not competent
- He asked God to send someone to accompany him in his mission [324]

Despite his reluctance to lead, Moses is recognized as a pivotal historical figure in both a religious and social context. He is central to three of the world's major religions — Judaism, Christianity and Islam — as well as to many other religions in the world.[325] In the New Testament, Moses is mentioned over 80 times, which is more than any other figure in the Hebrew Bible. Moses, the "confidant of God," is mentioned in 34 chapters of the Koran, which is more than a quarter of the total.[326] The Law of Moses is generally summarized as the worship of a single, invisible and just God with the rejection of every form of idolatry and paganism.

But the message goes beyond religious observance to deal with political, social and family affairs. Moses established the absence of an arbitrary exercise of power — that even a king must fear God and obey the law. He taught that justice must be impartially administered, for rich and poor alike, but that special protection is to be offered to the needy or underprivileged. He insisted we respect women, employ fair practices in

---

[324] Terrence E. Fretheim, *Interpretation: A Bible Commentary for Teaching and Preaching Exodus*, (Louisville, Ky: John Knox Press, 1991), 52.
[325] Rabbi Levi Meier, PhD, *Moses--The Prince, the Prophet: His Life, Legend & Message for Our Lives*, (Woodstock, Vt.: Jewish Lights Publishing, 1999), 2.
[326] Bruce Feiler, *America's Prophet: Moses and the American Story*, (New York: HarperCollins Publishers, 2009), 20.

commerce and exempt certain men from military service.[327] Moses' life includes many profound examples of how personal struggle against terrible odds can bring about liberation and change.

The story of Moses begins in the Book of Exodus, Chapter 2. His birth and childhood demonstrate his divine ability to prevail and set the stage for his achievements later in life. Moses was born to a family of Hebrew slaves in Egypt at a time when the pharaoh was determined to eliminate them. Although the Israelites were only a small fraction of the many slaves held captive in Egypt, the pharaoh was concerned because the number of Hebrews was steadily increasing.[328] He worried that as their population grew, the Israelites might join forces with an approaching invader and rebel against the Egyptians.[329] As a result, the pharaoh devised a plan to eliminate the Hebrews by increasing the severity of their forced labor and ordering the death of all their newborn male children.[330] At the time of Moses' birth, the Israelites were required to cast their newborn males into the Nile River. Moses' mother ignored this command and hid him from the Egyptians.

When Moses was about 3 months old, his mother could no longer safely conceal him. In a show of great faith, she found a way to technically comply with the pharaoh's command without drowning her son.[331] She crafted an ark of reeds to float on the water; she placed him into the basket on the river's edge. Moses' sister Miriam kept watch over his basket from a distance until it was discovered by one of the pharaoh's own daughters, who had come down to bathe in the river. Although the princess recognized that he was a Hebrew, she took pity on the baby and adopted him as her own. When Miriam saw this, she came forward and suggested that the princess hire a Hebrew woman to nurse the child. The princess agreed, and sent Miriam to find a nursemaid. Miriam quickly returned with Moses' own mother, who was then hired

---

327 Joan Comay, *Who's Who in the Old Testament*, (New York: Routledge, 2002), 254.
328 Henry Enoch Kagan, *Six who changed the world: Moses, Jesus, Paul, Marx, Freud, Einstein*, (New York : Thomas Yoseloff, 1963), 49.
329 Ibid.
330 Ibid.
331 Carl S. Ehrlich, "Moses, Torah, and Judaism," *Moses, Buddha, Confucius, Jesus, and Muhammad as Religious Founders*, Edited by David Noel Freedman and Michael J. McClymond, forward by Hans Kung, (Grand Rapids, Mich.: William B. Eerdmans Publishing Company, 2001), 49.

to care for him during his early years.[332] When he was old enough to eat solid food, Moses' mother brought him back to the princess just as she had promised. Thereafter, the princess raised him as if he were her own child.[333]

The great Biblical stories of Moses' life commence when he is a young man venturing from the palace for the first time. Jewish legend then continues Moses' story, describing a number of events concerning his childhood. Among the most notable is one that occurred during his earliest years at the palace.

The pharaoh reportedly favored Moses among the grandchildren, despite warnings from his prophets that Moses would one day destroy him. So the pharaoh asked them to devise a test to provide evidence of Moses' threat. The prophets presented Moses with two baskets, the first filled with fine jewels and the second with burning coals. It was said that if Moses reached for the jewels, it would be a sign of his intent to overthrow the pharaoh. But if he reached instead for the hot coals, it would be a sign of his innocence and he would be permitted to live.

When presented with the baskets, Moses initially began to reach for the jewels. Jewish legend explains how an angel of the Lord stopped him and pushed his hand into the burning coals. Touching them, he immediately brought his fingers to his mouth in an effort to cool the burn. As he did, he burned his lips and tongue, causing him to stutter and have difficulty speaking throughout the remainder of his lifetime.[334] His sacrifice, however, won the pharaoh's trust.

Moses grew up at the palace with all the privileges and luxuries of an Egyptian prince. As he matured, he remained a favorite of the pharaoh, and was eventually appointed overseer of the entire household. Rabbi Levi Meier, Ph.D., speculates that Moses was most likely exposed to constant criticism of the enslaved Israelites while he was pampered and isolated with the other princes and princesses. Even Egyptian artifacts from this period depict the slaves as being different from the Egyptians, to the extent that they are considered not quite human, with cheap and expendable lives.[335] Dr. Henry Enoch Kagan, a theologian and psychologist, theorizes that Moses must have felt rejected by his

---

[332] Ibid.
[333] Eric A. Kimmel, *Be Not Far From Me: The Oldest Love Story Legends from the Bible,* (New York: Simon and Schuster, 1998), 67.
[334] Ibid.
[335] Meier, Ibid, 20.

Hebrew birth family even though his mother had given him up only to save his life.[336] Kagan contends that Moses must have dealt with an inner emotional struggle stemming from his position as the adopted child of an unwed Egyptian princess, and that it was this inner struggle — whether to be a loyal Egyptian or a loyal Hebrew — that helped form his character as an adult.[337]

In time, Moses left the comfort of the palace to go out into society to see the plight of the Hebrew slaves firsthand.[338] At this point, the Bible resumes the story of Moses' life. It begins in the book of Exodus with the description of an event that illustrates Moses' compassion toward the oppressed:

> One day, when Moses had grown up, he went out to
> his people and looked on their burdens; and he saw an
> Egyptian beating a Hebrew, one of his people. He
> looked this way and that, and seeing no one, he killed
> the Egyptian and hid him in the sand.

From these first words describing Moses as an adult, it is clear that he was a man who showed care and concern for others, who sided with the oppressed and who was ready and willing to take swift and decisive action to correct an injustice.[339] Although Moses himself had nothing to gain by getting involved with the slaves and their problems, he had a passion for justice and for defending the rights of the weak and downtrodden.[340] This story establishes Moses' connection with his people and illustrates his willingness to intervene to help them.[341]

Before killing the Egyptian, it is unclear if Moses was looking about in hopes that someone else would appear and intervene on his behalf or to determine if the coast was clear before taking action.[342] Either way, the biblical account continues with the betrayal of Moses by the very people he was attempting to protect.[343] Shortly after he killed the

---

[336] Kagan, Ibid, 54.
[337] Ibid, 53.
[338] Ibid.
[339] Harold S. Kushner, *Overcoming Life's Disappointments*, (New York: First Anchor Books, a division of Random House, 2006), 9.
[340] Ehrlich, 59.
[341] Kushner, 9.
[342] Ibid.
[343] Ehrlich, 58.

Egyptian, Moses came upon two Hebrews fighting and confronted the one who had unjustly attacked the other.[344] This brief incident reaffirms Moses' compassion for the oppressed, no matter who was harming them.[345] It also explains why Moses left his life as an Egyptian prince and fled from the only home he had ever known.[346]

Rather than backing off, the guilty slave turned to Moses and taunted him. The aggressor asked why Moses thought he was their ruler and threatened to expose him for killing the Egyptian.[347] In his book, *Six Who Changed the World*, Kagan recognizes this man's reaction as an indication of the rejection Moses may have often felt from the Hebrews for being associated with the Egyptians.[348] After the incident, Moses knew he was no longer safe in Egypt. Not only was he shunned by the Hebrew people, but now the pharaoh would also likely order the Egyptians to kill him upon discovering what Moses had done to the Egyptian taskmaster.

According to the biblical narrative, Moses feared for his safety and left Egypt quickly after his encounter with the Hebrew slaves. He headed east until he arrived in Midian, where Moses once again came to the aid of those needing assistance. Seven daughters of a Midian priest were gathered at a well to draw water for their father's sheep when Moses witnessed shepherds molesting the women. He chased off the attackers and stayed to help the sisters water their flock.[349] Moses showed that he was willing to stand up for the weak and oppressed, even when they were not his own people.[350] He chose to get involved, and he dealt swiftly and decisively with the injustice.[351] In return, the sisters brought Moses to the tent of their father, the priest, after their rescue. Welcoming and thanking Moses, the priest offered his daughter's hand in marriage.[352] In return, Moses promised to never take his bride, Zipporah, away from her father's home. Moses and Zipporah had two sons and lived with Zipporah's father for many years.

---

344 Ibid.
345 Meier, Ibid, 24.
346 Erlich, 59.
347 Kagan, Ibid, 56.
348 Ibid.
349 Meier, 27.
350 Kimmel, 69.
351 Meier, 27.
352 Ehrlich, 59.

During his time in Midian, Moses tended to the flocks of his father-in-law. His life as a shepherd provides one of many examples in the Bible when God tests a man in little things before giving him an important task.[353]

Moses showed meticulous concern for the safety and wellness of each animal and took them to pasture in a manner designed to benefit the entire flock. First, he led the youngest animals, so that they could eat the tender, juicy grass. Next, he allowed the somewhat older animals to graze. Finally, he brought the healthy grown sheep to eat the remaining grass, which provided good food for them but could not be eaten by the other sheep.[354] According to Jewish legend, Moses once saw a little lamb wandering away from the others. He quickly followed until the lamb stopped to drink at a small stream. The legend continues that Moses waited for the lamb to finish and then picked it up and carried it back to the others. As he did, Moses apologized to the lamb, explaining he would have carried the lamb to the water himself if he had known it was thirsty. Stories like these explain how God recognized Moses' care and concern for all the sheep.[355]

God concluded that Moses would exercise the same care for His people, and He appeared to Moses on the mountainside. Moses noticed a strange flame emerging from a bush that was burning, but was not consumed by the fire.[356] Once again, he demonstrated his readiness to get involved by taking the time and effort to investigate the burning bush.[357] When Moses approached, God revealed Himself in the bush and charged Moses with confronting the pharaoh in order to lead the Israelites out of Egypt.[358] God's voice addressed Moses and explained that He had witnessed the oppression and the cries of the Israelites, and He wanted Moses to free His people.[359] One would expect Moses to have been overjoyed at the prospect of serving God, but his first instinct was to plead inadequacy, saying: "Who am I that I should go to Pharaoh and free the Israelites from Egypt?" (Exodus 3:11)

---

353 Louis Ginzberg, The *Legends of the Jews, Bible Times and Characters, Volume 4*, (Echo Library, 2007), 29.
354 Ibid.
355 Meier, Ibid, 31.
356 Ibid.
357 Ibid.
358 Ehrlich, Ibid, 69.
359 Kagan, Ibid.

But in the end, Moses accepted the mission. To give him further strength and confidence, God empowered him with the ability to perform certain wonders. First, Moses was able to change his rod into a snake by casting it onto the ground; when he reached down to catch the snake by its tail, it became a rod again in his hand. Next, Moses put his hand into his robe, and when he took it out, it was leprous and diseased; putting his hand back into his robe and removing it, the hand was restored to healthy flesh. Finally, God told Moses that if the pharaoh did not believe these signs or listen to him, Moses would be able to take water from the Nile and pour it onto the ground, where it would become blood.

Even with these advantages, Moses continued to show humility and a sense of unworthiness.[360] At times, he still pleaded with God to be released from the assignment and complained that he was not a strong speaker. God finally became angry with Moses and commanded him to accept the mission, along with the assurance that his brother Aaron would speak for him.[361] Moses then committed himself fully to the task, dedicating his life to its achievement. In return, God explained the coming course of events. He instructed Moses to go before the pharaoh to ask him to release the Israelites, but God also warned that the pharaoh would not agree until he was compelled to do so. God promised to stay with Moses throughout his mission and promised to torment all of Egypt until the pharaoh agreed to let the Israelites go.

At God's instruction, Moses and Aaron assembled the elders of Israel before going to meet with the pharaoh. They relayed His message and demonstrated the wonders that He had empowered them to perform.[362] Believing that God had heard their prayers, the elders and the people of Israel accepted Moses as their leader and promised to follow him wherever he led.[363] Meier identifies the support that Moses received from his family and his people as the source for the inner strength he found to proceed.[364] Moses, Aaron and the elders set out to meet with Pharaoh. Along the way, the elders lost their courage; one by one they dropped behind and went home. By the time Moses and Aaron

---

360 Ehrlich, Ibid, 62.
361 Kagan, Ibid.
362 Meier, Ibid.
363 Kimmel, Ibid.
364 Meier, Ibid.

finally arrived at the palace gate, they stood alone.[365] Yet Moses did not lose faith. Rather than turning back with the elders, he proceeded on his mission and went to the pharaoh to seek release of God's people.

On his first attempt to convince the pharaoh to release the Israelites, Moses requested only a three-day journey to allow his people to go into the wilderness and worship their God.[366] After much deliberation, the pharaoh actually granted permission but with an important condition—the Hebrew women and children would have to remain behind as hostages.[367] Moses refused to compromise, a decision that had drastic, immediate consequences.[368] The pharaoh accused the Israelites of trying to avoid their duties, and commanded that their workload be increased.[369] Also, to punish Moses for inspiring the slaves with dreams of freedom, the pharaoh tried to weaken Moses' leadership position and turn the Hebrews against him. He ordered that the Hebrew slaves no longer be given straw to make their bricks.[370] Instead, they would have to gather their own straw, while their daily quota for brick production remained unchanged. To make matters worse, the Egyptian landowners chased the Israelites from the fields where they tried to gather straw; then they beat them for not producing as many bricks as they previously had.[371]

Even though he knew how the pharaoh would respond to his request, Moses still had a difficult time accepting the outcome of his first intervention.[372] The Israelites worked hard trying to meet the pharaoh's impossible new goals, but they were — of course — unsuccessful;[373] and the slaves turned on Moses and attacked him for being the cause of their additional suffering.[374] Not only was the pharaoh opposed to him, but now Moses' own people — the ones on whose behalf he was supposedly working — had also rejected him.[375] Moses asked God why he had been chosen for this failed mission and why God had allowed the Israelites'

---

365 Kimmel, Ibid.
366 Kagan, Ibid.
367 Ibid.
368 Meier, Ibid.
369 Ehrlich, Ibid, 71.
370 Meier, Ibid.
371 Meier, Ibid, 80.
372 Ibid, 61.
373 Ibid.
374 Ehrlich, Ibid, 71.
375 Ehrlich, Ibid, 72.

condition to worsen.[376] He asked how it would ever be possible for him to persuade the pharaoh when he could not even convince his own people to listen to him.[377] God appeared to Moses again, reminding him of the unbreakable covenant He had given His people and reassuring him that God would fulfill His promise.[378] Moses conveyed God's pledge to the Israelites, but they could not even listen to this message of hope. The spirit of the slaves was so crushed, and they were so exhausted from their labors that no words could comfort them.[379] Instead, they cursed Moses and complained that his interference was only making things worse.[380]

Moses did not lose faith, however, and he and Aaron appeared before the pharaoh once again at the command of God. Moses knew that the pharaoh still would not agree to his request, but he and Aaron intended to demonstrate the divine powers God had given them. Just as God had predicted, the pharaoh asked Moses and Aaron to prove themselves to him by working a miracle. On Moses' command, Aaron cast down his rod, which immediately turned into a serpent. The pharaoh responded by summoning his magicians, who did the same with their rods. Aaron reached down to pick up the serpent, and it immediately turned back into a rod. The pharaoh's magicians did the same. But then the rod of Aaron and Moses came to life and swallowed the rods of all the magicians.[381] The pharaoh was still not convinced, however, and refused to release the Israelites. As a result, God brought on a series of 10 plagues that were calculated to break the willpower of the pharaoh and his followers.[382]

Before each of the first nine plagues, Moses asked the pharaoh to release the Israelites. Each time, Moses warned the pharaoh of the impending tragedy that would occur if he refused to honor the request. Nine times the pharaoh turned Moses away; nine times each denial was followed by the next in the series of plagues, just as Moses had warned. The water of the Nile turned to blood; the land of Egypt was infested with frogs; the dust in the air turned into a mass of gnats; animals from

---

376 Meier, Ibid, 60.
377 Ehrlich, Ibid, 72.
378 Meier, Ibid, 61.
379 Ibid.
380 Kushner, Ibid, 16.
381 Meier, Ibid, 62.
382 Ehrlich, Ibid, 73.

the wilderness harassed the Egyptians; an epidemic disease killed Egyptian livestock; incurable boils afflicted the Egyptian people; a powerful storm destroyed fields, crops, livestock and people; swarms of locusts consumed all the remaining Egyptian crops; and total darkness fell upon the land.

The plagues created a steadily increasing burden on the Egyptians, and the pharaoh tried compromising with Moses as they continued. Moses, however, refused to compromise and never altered his request. Throughout each plague, the pharaoh eventually consented to let the Israelites leave in exchange for an end to the current plague. But time and time again, he refused to honor his agreement when the plague was lifted. This pattern continued for each of the first nine plagues, until the pharaoh was personally affected by the death of his firstborn son and feared his own death during the 10th and final plague.

Before the last plague, Moses did not ask the pharaoh again to set the Hebrews free. Instead, he simply explained what was about to happen: The 10th plague would cause the death of the firstborn child in every Egyptian home.[383] Moses told the pharaoh that only the children of Israel would be safe, because God could tell the difference between Egypt and Israel. He predicted that the pharaoh's subjects would come running to Moses and beg him to take his people away from Egypt. Moses did not wait for the pharaoh's response, but instead turned and walked away without looking back.[384] Moses knew that the pharaoh himself would seek him out during the night and urge him to leave with the Israelites as quickly as possible. Moses, however, chose to show continued respect to the pharaoh by mentioning only that the servants of the ruler would beg for Moses and the Israelites to leave, and not the pharaoh himself.[385]

Through Moses, God instructed the Israelites to prepare for the 10th plague and to demonstrate their commitment to Him. The Egyptians practiced idolatry, which included worship of the ram.[386] But on the night of the 10th plague, every Hebrew household was instructed to slaughter a sacrificial lamb for a final meal. The ceremony of the Israelites provided an opportunity for God's people to demonstrate that

383 Kushner, Ibid, 17.
384 Kimmel, Ibid, 77.
385 Ginzberg, Ibid, 58.
386 Ibid, 59.

they were rejecting the Egyptian gods and displaying obedience to the God of Israel.[387] The very act of slaughtering an Egyptian deity showed the Israelites' growing confidence in gaining their freedom. Moses had earned their support and inspired strength and hope in his followers.

As an outward symbol of their commitment to God, each Israelite household also took the blood from the sacrificial lamb and smeared it on their doorposts, where it would be visible to all. While the Israelites were chosen for God's salvation, everyone could participate in eating the sacrifice — men, women, Israelites, strangers and converts.[388] Anyone who was willing to accept the God of Israel was welcomed to follow Moses. God asked that this night be remembered with the celebration of a similar feast each year on the anniversary of the 10th plague. This tradition is known as the Jewish Passover, because the 10th plague "passed over" the Israelite homes, which were identified by the blood of the lamb.

Just as Moses had predicted, the pharaoh's own people came and begged the pharaoh to release the Hebrew slaves during the night of the final plague.[389] The pharaoh agreed, in part because he was a firstborn son and afraid that death would strike him down, too.[390] Promptly, he went to Moses and urged him to lead the Israelites away from Egypt immediately. The Egyptians gave the slaves gifts of sheep, oxen, gold and fine jewels to take with them. As joyful as the Israelites were to be delivered from the Egyptian bondage, the pharaoh's people were even happier to see them leave. In fact, the pharaoh and his people quickly helped the Israelites load their possessions in order to get them out of the land as quickly as possible.[391] The dread of death, which had obsessed the Egyptians, left with the departing Hebrews.[392]

On their journey, the Israelites seemed to forget, almost immediately, just how hard life had been in Egypt. When they had been out of Egypt for only three days, Moses followed God's command to "turn back" and encamp by the sea. Meanwhile, the pharaoh had experienced a change of heart and joined in the pursuit of the Israelites with a large army. Pharaoh rejoiced to see that the Israelites had turned

---

[387] Meier, Ibid, 89.
[388] Ibid.
[389] Kagan, Ibid, 67.
[390] Ginzberg, Ibid, 63.
[391] Ginzberg, 63.
[392] Ibid, 64.

back, and he planned his attack.[393] The Israelites were camped beside the Red Sea with no way to cross when they looked up and saw a cloud of dust rising in the distance. As the cloud came nearer, they realized it was the pharaoh and his chariot army bearing down on them.[394] The Israelites blamed Moses instantly, accusing him of leading them into the desert to die and saying that they would have been better off remaining as slaves in Egypt. Yet Moses did not lose faith. He led them into the Red Sea with a promise that God would part the waters for them to cross safely.

Despite all the miracles they had already witnessed, the Israelites were reluctant to follow Moses at the sea. Faith requires action to be sustained, and none of them was willing to take that first step into the waters.[395] Finally, one man demonstrated his absolute faith by entering the raging waters. As everyone else watched, the sea continued to swirl and rise around him, until Moses stretched his hand over the waters as God had commanded. The sea then began to part, and the Israelites were able to cross safely.[396] The pharaoh and his chariots charged after them, but the undersea path was slick with mud and choked with sharp stones,[397] and the wheels of the pharaoh's chariots sank in the marshland and became stuck.[398] Once more, Moses stretched his hand over the sea as God had commanded. With that, the waters crashed down on the pharaoh and his entire pursing army, drowning all of them.[399]

Moses had finally achieved the first step in his mission to lead God's people into the Promised Land. He had been able to gain enough of their trust and confidence to unite them and bring them out of Egypt. With the danger of Pharaoh and his pursuing army now eliminated, the people turned their fears toward the responsibilities that come with freedom. The Israelites actually seemed to prefer the routine and security of slavery to the risks of being free.[400] At least in Egypt, they had the certainty of being fed every day. As free people, they were now

---

393 Meier, Ibid, 102.
394 Kimmel, Ibid, 79.
395 Meier, Ibid, 104.
396 Meier, Ibid, 106.
397 Kimmel, Ibid, 81.
398 Kagan, Ibid, 70.
399 Meier, Ibid, 106.
400 Ibid, 120.

responsible for locating and retrieving their own food and water.[401] They lacked the confidence of knowing where their next meal would come from, and they longed for the "security" that came with being slaves. When things became difficult or uncertain, they quickly turned on Moses and complained about their hardships.

The first complaints were in regard to their need for drinking water. For three days after crossing the Red Sea, they had no water to drink. Arriving at Marah, they found water but soon discovered it wasn't fit to drink. They quickly went from singing praises to God to expressing fear, confusion and bewilderment.[402] They immediately began to complain to Moses, crying in desperation and accusing him of bringing them out of Egypt to die of thirst in the desert.[403] Moses remained calm and confident. He did not yell or berate the people. Instead, he asked God for guidance and direction.[404] He prayed and followed God's instruction to take a branch from the laurel tree and throw it into the well.[405] The branch made the bitter water drinkable, and the Israelites were able to quench their thirst as they praised God.

Resuming their journey, the Israelites once again revealed their fear when water was not available, and their thirst became severe.[406] Instead of searching for new springs and trying to solve the problem, the Israelites hurried to Moses and demanded water to drink.[407] This time, Moses was angered and asked the people why they were complaining to him. He told them to take their concerns directly to God and to stop looking to Moses to provide everything for them.

In spite of their lack of faith, Moses still responded to the people's request for water. He prayed for a source of water, and the Lord told Moses to strike his staff against a rock. As soon as the staff struck the rock, water flowed freely. Once again God provided for the Israelites.

Despite God's repeated answers to their prayers, the Israelites kept complaining, and they turned on Moses with anger and fear each time they faced difficulty.[408] When the food and provisions brought from

---

401 Ibid.
402 Meier, Ibid, 117.
403 Kimmel, Ibid, 81.
404 Meier, Ibid, 117.
405 Kimmel, Ibid, 81.
406 Meier, Ibid, 119.
407 Kimmel, Ibid, 83.
408 Ibid.

Egypt had run out, the Israelites found themselves in the wilderness with no native vegetation or crops to provide sustenance. Again, the Israelites looked back on their days of slavery in Egypt with longing.[409] They did not seem to recall the beatings or the oppression by the Egyptians but spoke instead of the wonderful meals they had been fed. Their memories were highly selective, and the people were convinced that whatever they might have experienced in Egypt was better than a slow, torturous death by starvation.[410] The first pangs of hunger quickly transformed Moses in their eyes from a heroic liberator into an evil villain.[411]

But the people were not destined to starve in the desert. Once again, Moses brought their concerns before God, and God responded. Each morning, "bread" — manna — rained down from Heaven for the Israelites.[412] Moses announced the coming miracle to his followers and explained one simple rule for the manna: the Israelites must trust God to provide for them every day.[413] God began to establish some expectations for his followers to demonstrate their commitment to Him. Every morning, the Israelites were to go out before sunrise and gather enough manna to feed their household for one day. When the sun came up, the manna melted away. Anyone who did not go out early was without bread on that day. At the same time, no manna could be saved to eat the following day. Moses explained that going out each morning to gather manna for the day was a way for the Israelites to show their faith in God.

However, the people demonstrated that they were still not quite ready for this show of faith. Some of them stored away extra manna, only to find it stinking, rotting and crawling with worms the next day.[414] Understandably, Moses became frustrated and angry with the Israelites, and God responded with yet another miracle. Moses warned his followers that no manna would fall on the Sabbath. He told them to gather twice as much manna as usual the day before, promising it would not rot or become infested overnight.[415] Despite these instructions, some

---

[409] Ibid.
[410] Meier, Ibid, 123.
[411] Meier, Ibid, 122.
[412] Meier, Ibid, 123.
[413] Meier, Ibid, 124.
[414] Kimmel, Ibid, 83.
[415] Kimmel, Ibid, 83.

people still went out on the morning of the Sabbath to search for manna.[416] But those who demonstrated their faith found that the manna they saved from the day before remained as fresh as it was when gathered. Through consistency and repetition, Moses introduced a shift in perspective for the Israelites. He demonstrated that the way to faith involves living in the present and not constantly worrying about what has been or might be.[417] Moses remained steadfast and optimistic in his leadership by constantly taking the concerns of his followers before God and continuing to demonstrate his obedience and faith.

According to Kagan, the supreme task of Moses was to change a frightened tribe wandering without a goal into a people filled with a fighting courage because they had a destiny. In his book *The Prince, The Prophet,* Meier also points out that the struggles facing the Israelites extended far beyond the initial concerns for their physical needs. They also struggled with a fundamental, non-material concern dealing with the duality of human nature — good vs. evil. Meier recognizes Moses as a great, inspired leader who set about the difficult challenge of instructing his followers in how to overcome the "bad" with "good." Meanwhile, the frightened behavior of these followers repeatedly tested Moses and brought him to the edge of giving up.[418] Rather than bear the burden of continuing to care for these people on his own, Moses begged God to take his life. He reminded God that he neither conceived the people nor chose to lead them. They were the chosen responsibility of God, not Moses.[419]

As part of successfully leading the Israelites to God's Promised Land, Moses was also responsible for transforming the frightened followers into a united people with a sense of purpose and destiny. Attacks on the Hebrews by outsiders helped serve this purpose by bringing Moses' followers together in a united defense. Neighboring nations had all learned of the Israelites' miraculous deliverance from the mighty Egyptian empire and of the series of plagues leading to their escape. Some tribes extended hospitality to the marching Israelites while others blocked their path and had to be subdued in combat.[420]

---

[416] Meier, Ibid, 124.
[417] Ibid.
[418] Kagan, Ibid, 76.
[419] Ehrlich, Ibid, 106.
[420] Kagan, Ibid, 72.

One of the greatest threats to the Hebrews came from the nation of Amalek.[421]

The Amalekites did not share the values of the Israelites, and they began a confrontation by wiping out the weak and weary Israelites who lagged behind the main columns.[422] Moses appointed his deputy, Joshua, to lead the counterattack. In his book, *Be Not Far From Me*, Eric A. Kimmel explains that Moses knew Joshua would be better suited to lead the Israelite soldiers into battle because he was far younger and stronger than Moses. Moses took up a position overlooking the battlefield where he could pray for and watch over the Israelites in battle. From this vantage point, Moses remained a dedicated leader. As the warring Israelites gazed up at him, Moses lifted his hands and inspired them to defeat the Amalekites.[423] When the people looked to Moses, they saw not only the man, but also his accomplishments and everything that he stood for.[424] Meier describes Moses' hands as symbols of God's presence and power.

The manner in which Moses held his hands seemed to have a direct influence on the success of the Israelites on the battlefield. When Moses held his hands high for the Israelites to see, his followers gained strength and confidence in their fight against the Amalekites. But when Moses grew tired and lowered his hands, the Israelites lost faith and the Amalekites gained power.

Moses' trusted supporters, Aaron and Hur, came to his aid. They brought a stone for him to sit upon and stood at his side to support his hands when they became heavy.[425] With the help of Aaron and Hur, Moses kept his hands steady and high until the eventual Israelite victory.

After defeating the Amalekites, the Israelites continued through the wilderness and camped at the base of Mt. Sinai. Moses' father-in-law heard that they were staying at the mountain under Moses' leadership, and he brought Zipporah and Moses' sons with him to join the Israelites. From the moment he accepted his position, Moses had focused on his

---

[421] Meier, Ibid, 128.
[422] Ehrlich, Ibid, 85.
[423] Meier, Ibid, 130.
[424] Ibid, 131.
[425] Ibid.

singular mission. He did not let the people's doubt and fear affect his own high level of optimism and confidence.[426]

With the permission of his father-in-law, Moses had put his mission to save the Israelites ahead of the needs of his wife and their two sons.[427] He kept his promise not to take Zipporah away from her father's home when he first set out to return to Egypt and confront the pharaoh. As he did so, Moses devoted total, constant and complete dedication to his mission.

Moses provided his followers with the framework for a higher religious life and moral culture.[428] He embodied an attitude and set of behaviors that provided a natural example of the "righteous" way to walk through life.[429] Remarkably, Moses found the ability — and the desire — to go on leading a fearful, anxious people, whose constant refrain was essentially, "Let us return to Egypt."[430]

The journey from Egypt to Mt. Sinai took seven weeks, and not much had been required of the people as a whole during that time.[431] They had primarily been passive observers, not active participants.[432] The people began this journey timid and afraid, without adequate faith to sustain them during periods of difficulty.[433] Even when they were engaged in battle with the Amalekites, they had to look to Moses' uplifted hands to gain the necessary strength to overcome the enemy.[434]

The people's dependence on Moses continued at the base of Mt. Sinai, where hundreds of them lined up before him every day to ask his advice and guidance on a wide range of issues and problems, domestic disputes and ethical questions. Because the people were bringing every little dispute before Moses, his father-in law noted that he would soon exhaust himself trying to settle all these matters. Furthermore, the Israelites would never learn to govern themselves with Moses presiding over every question and concern.

Moses' success leading the Israelites away from Egypt and out of slavery had simply been the first step toward delivering them into

---

[426] Meier, Ibid, 140.
[427] Ibid, 135.
[428] Ehrlich, Ibid, 21.
[429] Meier, Ibid, 138.
[430] Ibid, 139.
[431] Ibid.
[432] Meier, Ibid, 144.
[433] Ibid, 139.
[434] Ibid.

freedom. True liberation required teaching and instructions for how to govern and provide for themselves. At his father-in-law's suggestion, Moses appointed highly qualified officers to govern the people and judge the small matters.[435]

This system greatly eased Moses' burden. The people brought their concerns to Moses' officers, and Moses heard only the larger matters and disputes. Meanwhile, he continued to show remarkable dedication to his followers, demonstrating how they should relate to one another in a caring, compassionate manner. Slowly, the people learned to change their behavior.[436]

The transformations that the Israelites experienced in the wilderness before reaching Mt. Sinai and the wisdom they acquired while camped at the base of the mountain, prepared them to receive the Ten Commandments and move closer toward freedom.[437] The mountain was covered with a thick cloud, which produced thunder, lightning and the loud blast of a trumpet. God came down under the cover of smoke to present the Ten Commandments to the people.[438]

Moses' leadership had a positive effect on the Israelites, and they accepted God's covenant at the base of Mt. Sinai. This formal relationship was based on the belief that God would care for the people of Israel in exchange for their devotion to Him.[439] This covenant and the imparting of the Ten Commandments became the central building blocks in the development of distinctly Jewish lifestyles through the ages.[440] When they promised to obey God's covenant, the Israelites also gave Moses their blessing and support to climb Mt. Sinai and speak with God face-to-face to receive their instructions. Moses left Aaron and Hur in charge and went to the top of the mountain to talk with God.

Moses remained at the summit of the mountain for 40 days. During this time, he received written instructions on the Ten Commandments and many other rules, ordinances and regulations for following God's direction.[441] Meanwhile, the Israelites grew restless as they camped at the foot of the mountain. They began to wonder if Moses would ever

---

435 Kimmel, Ibid, 84.
436 Meier, Ibid, 138.
437 Ibid, 141.
438 Comay, Ibid, 248.
439 Ehrlich, Ibid, 86.
440 Ehrlich, Ibid, 86.
441 Kimmel, Ibid, 86.

return. He had led them through every test and ordeal they had endured; with his absence, they began to fear that they had been abandoned.[442] The Israelites had already heard that they should have no other gods or make any graven images, and they had already proclaimed they would follow all of the commandments.[443] But fear overcame faith, and the Israelites went to Aaron and Hur, demanding that they make another god for them.[444]

So while Moses was at the top of Mt. Sinai receiving the instructions God had inscribed on the stone tablets, the people were at the base of the mountain already breaking their promise to follow God. Aaron tried to buy time before complying with the demands. He requested that the Israelites gather all their gold and bring it to him to construct the idol. He hoped the people would resist and Moses would return in time to intervene. But the people complied, and Aaron constructed a golden calf for the Israelites. Immediately, the people began worshipping the golden calf. They brought sacrifices, ate and drank and danced around the idol.[445]

When God saw this, He became furious. He told Moses that He would destroy the people and make a great new nation for Moses to lead.[446] Moses pleaded with God to have mercy and reminded Him of His promise to care for the people of Israel.[447] He pointed out that the Egyptians would gain strength if God let His anger destroy His people.[448] They would say God brought the Israelites out of slavery only to wipe them off the Earth.[449] Moses soothed God's anger; now he had to descend from the mountain and confront the sinners himself.[450]

When Moses came down from the mountain and actually saw what the people were doing, he was consumed by rage. He hurled down the stone tablets, which shattered into pieces.[451] He burned the golden statue in the fire, ground the cooled metal into powder, mixed the

---

442 Meier, Ibid, 151.
443 Ibid.
444 Kimmel, Ibid, 87.
445 Ibid, 88.
446 Ibid.
447 Ibid.
448 Ibid.
449 Meier, Ibid, 160.
450 Ibid.
451 Kimmel, Ibid, 89.

powder with water and forced the Israelites to drink the mixture.[452] Moses called for his followers to punish the guilty individuals who had broken their promise to God. He ordered his followers to kill those who had urged Aaron to make the golden calf and those who made sacrifices to it.[453] This painful experience left Moses with a sense of failure, and he returned to the top of the mountain in an effort to take responsibility for the actions of his people. Showing true leadership, he asked God to forgive the Israelites, offering his own life on their behalf. For Moses' sake, God forgave the people and asked Moses to return to them with a second set of stone tablets.

As they neared their destination, Moses sent out 12 scouts — one from each tribe — to investigate the Promised Land. The explorers all returned with reports that the land was fruitful and bountiful, but also that it was covered with fortified towns. Ten of the scouts were convinced they would never be able to conquer the land, and they created hysteria among the people.[454] Once again, they railed against God and Moses for bringing them out of the safety and security of slavery and demanded appointment of a new leader and a return to Egypt. Only two scouts optimistically recommended continuing, and they were threatened by the others with death. Nevertheless, these loyal scouts continued to support Moses' leadership and tried to reassure the mob.[455]

God reacted to the hysteria by threatening to wipe out the people and make a great nation of Moses, but Moses pleaded with God to back down, which He did. But in his text on Moses, Torah and Judaism, Dr. Carl S. Ehrlich wrote that God swore He would cause them to wander in the desert for 40 years as a consequence of their lack of faith. Ehrlich argues that this wandering was necessary to allow time for the whole generation that had come out of Egypt — the generation that had given Moses constant trouble on the long journey — to die off before they could enter God's Promised Land.[456] He speculates that only a new generation, born and raised in freedom, would be deserving of God's grace.[457]

---

452 Ibid.
453 Ibid.
454 Ehrlich, Ibid, 108.
455 Kagan, Ibid, 76.
456 Ibid, 73.
457 Ehrlich, Ibid, 108.

This new generation did not know the old life known by their parents. They were born into the revolution and knew only its spirit of freedom.[458] They had been hardened by the rigors of desert life and disciplined by the new laws Moses had taught them.[459] During the 38 years of the temporary settlement, Moses finally coalesced a disorganized rabble of former slaves into a united, determined people. He disciplined them by means of a new moral code, a new legal system, a new religion with a new ceremonial cult and a new idealism that replaced the tribal traditions with a new concept of a united nation with a historic destiny.[460] It was this generation that resumed the march toward the Promised Land. Once again the Israelites set out on a lengthy detour to prepare for the battle ahead. They were repeatedly attacked, and a number were killed along the way. But they continued onward.

Kimmel explains that Moses knew his time had come to die as they reached the journey's end.[461] Moses was now 120 years old; his job was done. He set out alone to the summit of Mount Nebo, where he looked out over the Promised Land before his death. Before making this final climb, Moses asked the children of Israel to gather around him. He blessed them and appointed Joshua as their new leader. Rather than focusing on himself or his own lack of opportunity to enter the Promised Land, Moses used his final days to enhance the strength, purpose and direction of his followers. He reminded them of how God had taken care of them on their long journey to the Promised Land and assured them that He would continue to care for them as they proceeded. Moses instructed his followers to continue teaching future generations about God's grace and His commandments. He emphasized that God's law is intended to give them freedom and a full life — not to hold them in bondage or oppression.

God's relationship to his chosen people through Moses was new. At times, Moses and his followers did not understand God's purpose in His actions. Moses, as the leader of the Israelites and spiritual liaison with God, served as a great inspiration and source for optimism. He trusted God's judgment and believed God's blessings would carry the Jews through all hardships.

---

458 Kagan, Ibid, 73.
459 Comay, Ibid, 252.
460 Kagan, Ibid, 72.
461 Kimmel, Ibid, 90.

Unfortunately, Moses' followers were at times people of little faith. It was Moses' steadfast optimism that held the tribes together even as they were creating and worshiping images of pagan gods. The optimism instilled by Moses has found a permanent home with Muslims, Christians and Jews and their powerful, everlasting faith.

# BELVA ANN LOCKWOOD

Ten-year-old Belva Ann Bennett was certainly serious minded about her Christian faith. She truly believed that through faith, anything is possible. So, this 19th century tomboy decided to put her faith to the test. First, she attempted to walk on water as Jesus had done. She only got wet. When a young girl on a neighboring farm died, Belva attempted to raise her from the dead through deep concentration. But as hard as she tried, she could not bring the little girl back.[462]

Belva refused to be defeated by these two experiences. She simply decided to tackle something a little easier. Belva had also read in the Bible that just the faith of a tiny mustard seed could move a mountain. So, the Niagara County, New York, farm girl found a hill, sat down nearby and attempted to move the modest elevation of earth using her will alone. Once again, she failed.[463]

But from her three failed biblical tests of faith, Belva learned two valuable lessons in optimism. First, she confirmed that she did not have the power to raise the dead, but she was certain she could wake the living. And second, while faith was not enough to move a mountain— or even a small plateau— Belva realized a hill can be moved—with supreme optimism and one shovelful of earth at a time.[464]

When she grew up, Belva Bennett Lockwood would use her steel-toed faith to challenge a host of prejudices and inequities confronting Victorian-era women. Lockwood led the way in breaking down barriers in education, politics, and the practice of law.

Belva alone ripped down more barriers than 10 suffragettes combined. Her accomplishments seem endless. Belva earned a college degree, almost unheard of in those days. She taught school and became a principal. As a progressive educator, she founded the first successful school for girls and boys in Washington, D.C. She ran for U.S. President twice. She finished law school and had to fight her alma mater to receive

---

[462] Drollene P. Brown, *Belva Lockwood Wins Her Case*, (Morton Grove, Illinois: Albert Whitman & Company, 1987), 7.
[463] Ibid.
[464] Ibid.

the degree she had earned. She was the first American female allowed to practice law before the U.S. Supreme Court. She became a prominent attorney, winning a multi-million dollar lawsuit against the federal government on behalf of the Cherokee, another oppressed group of Americans. She became a leading figure in an anti-war movement that was unable to stop The Great War.

And she achieved her goals while raising a child as a single parent and overcoming the loss of two husbands and other close family members. Despite the head-shaking disapproval of the straight-laced populace, Belva's optimism carried her onward to overcome every artificial barrier.

Born on October 24, 1830, Belva learned early about the limitations foisted upon women of that era. After finishing the eighth grade—the last grade for which free schooling was available—Belva asked her father for the money to continue her education. He refused, saying a woman did not need to go beyond the eighth grade because too much schooling turned girls into "old maids."[465]

Tomboy by nature, Belva claimed she could row a boat, ride a horse and perform the heavy labor to care for the family's farm animals as well as any male. She was strong and healthy and loved the outdoors.[466] It is no wonder that she rebelled at the suggestion that she was somehow inferior to any male on the planet.

While her father would not pay for higher education, he did agree to allow Belva to go to private school— if she could pay her own way. Although only 14 years old and still a child herself, Belva obtained a job as a summer school teacher in nearby Royalton for $5 a week. Carefully saving every penny, Belva had enough money at the end of the summer to pay for a year's tuition at Girls' Academy, also located in Royalton.[467]

Achieving her dreams required constant effort. Belva worked extra hours doing household chores to pay for room and board in the boardinghouse where she was staying while attending school. Despite her heavy work load, she was also able to develop an active social life. She met a young farmer and sawmill worker named Uriah McNall, and they fell in love. He proposed marriage by the time she graduated from

---

[465] Ibid, 8.
[466] Jill Norgren, *Belva Lockwood: Equal Rights Pioneer*, (Minneapolis: Twenty-First Century Books, 2009), 13.
[467] Brown, Ibid, 9.

Girls' Academy in May 1848. They married in November 1848 and moved to Gasport where Uriah had a home.[468]

At last, Belva was conforming to Victorian family values. She bore a child in July 1849 and helped her husband run a sawmill in addition to farming. Unfortunately, tragedy arrived in the form of an industrial accident. Uriah was pinned under a number of falling logs being processed at the sawmill. He survived the accident but lapsed into a long period of declining health.[469] He never fully recovered from his injuries and died in his sleep on April 8, 1853. Some family members expressed a belief that Uriah had suffered from tuberculosis. He was only 28 and Belva 22. She would have to take care of her three-year-old child Lura as a single parent.[470]

Belva returned to the school where she had taught in the summer and asked for a full-time job. She was offered a job at $7 per week, the same salary she was paid as a part-time summer school teacher. She was experienced and had a degree, yet male teachers made between $10 and $15 a week for the same job. Belva turned down the job. When she related her experience to the wife of a minister in town, the woman said, "I cannot help you. You cannot help yourself. It is the way of the world."[471]

Just as Belva could not move a hill by wishing it away, she knew she could not remove this barrier without a tool. Belva decided the tool was education.[472] She made up her mind to do something about it.

First, she spent a year at Gasport Academy to brush up her education at Girls' Academy. After her mother Hannah agreed to keep Lura, Belva was able to attend Genessee Wesleyan Seminary in Lima, New York. Although a seminary school now refers to a religious school, in Belva's day, seminary meant a private school for young women.[473]

While friends and family discouraged Belva from going to school by telling her she was getting too much education, Belva felt just the opposite. She went to Genesee College, which would later become Syracuse University, and arranged to transfer there.[474] Energized by her

---

468 Ibid.
469 Ibid.
470 Ibid, 10.
471 Ibid, 12 — 13.
472 Ibid.
473 Ibid.
474 Ibid, 14.

high-voltage optimism, Belva decided to finish college in two years by going all year around. As she attended college, two other important issues began to surface for Belva.

The first one was women's rights, particularly the right to vote. In July 1848 in Seneca Falls, New York, about 100 men and women gathered for the first time in America's history for the sole purpose of "articulating female grievances and demanding women's equality."[475]

Sally G. McMillen, chairman of the history department at Davidson College, wrote in her recently published study of the women's rights event, *Seneca Falls and the Origins of the Women's Rights Movement*:

> Before Seneca Falls, no one could imagine that anyone would dare challenge, in such an organized manner, women's subservience or their legal, social, and political oppression. Before 1848, the nation's laws, traditions, and religious doctrines sustained women's subordinate status and codified their lack of legal and political rights. This Convention, though it lasted only two days, put everything into question and fostered a commitment to transform the country into a true democratic republic.[476]

Some of the most famous names in women's rights—both males and females—participated at the convention: Lucretia Mott, Elizabeth Cady Stanton, and abolitionist Frederick Douglass. While there had been little outcry— or even limited comment—about the plight of women, the Seneca Falls Convention changed all of that. The convention produced the "Declaration of Rights and Sentiments," which listed 18 injustices endured by women and a series of resolutions to address those wrongs. Women's rights became a major movement after the Seneca Falls Convention. Men and women began writing, lecturing and petitioning politicians to grant women full and equal rights enjoyed by all men.[477]

While some women, such as Susan B. Anthony and Lucy Stone, were seeking political solutions to the second-class status of women,

---

475 Sally G. McMillen, *Seneca Falls and the Origins of the Women's Rights Movement*, (New York: Oxford University Press, 2008), 3.
476 Ibid, 3 — 4.
477 Ibid, 4.

Belva was breaking down those barriers on her own. Using her optimism like a social sledgehammer, she had gone against the grain of Victorian society to obtain a college education. She was breaking down other doors of prejudice with her optimism.

And then, the second significant event occurred. Against the wishes of the college, she attended lectures by a lawyer in town. College officials deemed her presence "unladylike," but Belva had heard that excuse many times and never paid any attention to it.[478] These lectures may have planted the seed in Belva's mind about the value of a law degree.

When she graduated from college in June 1857, she was offered the job as principal of the Lockport, New York, Union School District. The specter of prejudice once again appeared to spread the virus of inequality. Even though Belva was in charge of all students and faculty, she was paid only $400 a year. Men teachers earned $600 without the major responsibilities Belva addressed.[479]

As principal of the school, Belva was able to make a difference to female students. She allowed girls to take public speaking classes, introduced them to gymnastics and took them on nature walks. She was able to obtain the approval of the school board despite objections by others.[480]

After four years at Lockport, she bought a school in Owego, New York. Ironically, had Belva been married, she would not have been able to buy property in her name. Because she was a widow, there was no legal reason for denying her the right to buy the school. Once again, Belva began providing new educational opportunities to female students with classes such as higher mathematics, gymnastics and public speaking.[481]

When the American Civil War began in 1861, Belva found herself torn between two causes. While she was anti-slavery, she was also anti-war. When the war ended in 1865 and slaves were freed throughout the country, Belva continued her interests in anti-war movements as well as the fight for women's rights.[482] She apparently realized, however, that the nation's capital was the place to effect changes. In February 1866,

---

[478] Brown, Ibid, 16.
[479] Ibid.
[480] Ibid, 17.
[481] Ibid, 18 – 19.
[482] Brown, Ibid, 20.

Belva and her 17-year-old daughter Lura moved to Washington, D.C., where Belva obtained a teaching position.

In the bustling city that housed America's executive, legislative and judicial branches of government, there were many things that attracted Belva's attention. She attended sessions of Congress and the Supreme Court. She studied international law. In her enthusiasm for government, she applied to fill a vacancy for a U.S. consul in the Belgium river port of Ghent. As might have been expected, her application was never even acknowledged.[483]

Despite the obvious disappointment, Belva never allowed the setback to dampen her optimism and spirit. She continued to read international law and studied German and Spanish in preparation for one day filling a foreign diplomatic role.[484]

Always the shrewd business woman, Belva apparently noticed the number of public meetings going on regarding issues such as temperance, women's rights, and world peace, to name a few. In 1867, she began buying public meeting halls and renting them for public meetings. One of her properties, Union League Hall on Ninth Street, became the meeting place for the Universal Franchise Association. The UFA was dedicated to bringing the vote to all men and women of all races. Belva became a vice president of the group.[485]

While active in the UFA, Belva met a dentist named Ezekiel Lockwood. She and Dr. Lockwood fell in love even though he was 28 years older than she. Nevertheless, they married on March 11, 1868. On January 28, 1869, a baby girl was born to the couple, and they named her Jessie. Having a child did not deter Belva from continuing her activities in support of women's rights. She and her husband joined a group called the National Woman Suffrage Association led by Susan B. Anthony and Elizabeth Cady Stanton. The goal of the group was to obtain an amendment to the U.S. Constitution recognizing women's right to vote.[486]

Belva was particularly troubled by the conditions women faced in domestic matters. A married woman was at the mercy of her husband and, in effect, had no rights in child custody or property ownership

---

483 Ibid, 21.
484 Ibid.
485 Ibid.
486 Ibid, 24.

matters. Women also were denied the best paying jobs or even the opportunity to get an education that would prepare them for professional positions. While she was active in presenting proposals to Congress, speaking on behalf of women, circulating petitions and attending women's rights conventions, she realized that the important step she must take was to enter law school.[487]

In October 1869, Belva attended two law school lectures at Columbian College in Washington, D.C. When she attempted to attend class a third time and offered to pay, her money was refused and she was instructed to apply to the faculty for admission. Two weeks after she applied, she received a reply which read, in part:

". . . [A]fter due consultation, have considered that such admission would not be expedient, as it would be likely to distract the attention of the young men."[488] The letter was signed by Dr. George W. Samson, president of the college. Despite her setback, Belva vowed to continue her efforts to study law.

Encouraged by her own optimism, Belva put her law school rejection behind her and began a new campaign in early 1870. This time she attempted to convince Congressmen to raise the wages for female government employees. Such a bill was introduced into the House by Samuel Arnell of Tennessee. Belva and Andrew Boyle, a member of Arnell's staff, actually drafted the legislation. Congressmen opposed to the bill argued that the only reason female workers were employed by the government was because they did not have to be paid as much as males. Arnell countered that women should receive the same pay for the same amount of work. Ultimately, a watered down version passed into law.[489]

More importantly, by constantly exceeding her grasp, Belva learned about politics, lobbyists and the ways of the world. Prize-winning legal historian Jill Norgren provides an insightful analysis of the importance of the congressional experience for Belva's professional growth:

> For Lockwood, lobbying the Arnell bill had been a
> difficult but thorough immersion in congressional
> politics. Through Boyle and Arnell she had gained

---

[487] Ibid.
[488] Ibid, 25.
[489] Norgren, *Equal Rights*, 47 – 48.

access to members of the House and Senate, and had won their respect for her advocacy work. Eight years later several of these congressmen would prove important in her fight to win women lawyers the right to practice in federal courts. Most critically, during the nearly four months in which the Arnell bill moved through Congress, she observed the game of political compromise first-hand. She learned that large principles often did not survive the play of politics but that a savvy representative could maneuver and win enactment of a more limited measure. This is just what Arnell had done. Broad principle was sacrificed in the name of a modest but nonetheless affirmative statement by Congress in the matter of equal employment rights.[490]

Belva was jubilant that she had struck a modest blow for women's rights, but her triumph was short lived. Tragically her 18-month-old infant Jessie contracted typhoid fever and died a few days later on July 28, 1870. The family was heart-broken, and Belva's smothering grief drove her into a short period of seclusion. Belva pulled herself out of her overwhelming sadness as she always had during previous times of grief—she concentrated on her work.[491]

And just as Belva's optimism carried her though difficult times in the past, it worked once again. Just a few months after Jessie's death, National University in Washington opened a law school, and the school's chancellor agreed to teach law to women. Belva and 14 other women enrolled in the two-year program. Their work load was the same as the men's. They attended lectures together, but they recited their lessons in private.[492]

The course was so difficult that all the other women dropped out except Belva and another student named Lydia Hall. They completed all requirements for graduation but were told a few weeks before the

---

490 Jill Norgren, *Belva Lockwood: The Woman Who Would Be President*, (New York: New York University Press, 2007), 7.
491 Brown, Ibid, 25 – 26.
492 Ibid, 26.

commencement exercises that they had not studied law long enough and would not receive their diplomas with the males.[493]

Both were outraged. In order to prove their legal competence, they sat for two days taking a special oral bar exam administered by the local bar association. Still they did not get their degrees. Lydia Hall gave up in anger and frustration. Belva, however, refused to give up. She sat for a second, three-day exam arranged by lawyer friends. The examining committee refused to issue a report.[494]

After a short trip to America's southern states to clear her head, Belva decided to obtain more legal training if that was what the examiners wanted. She asked to reapply to National University for more study, but she was denied.[495]

This time Belva appealed to President Ulysses S. Grant, who was also honorary president of the law school. She first wrote a long, detailed letter explaining her plight. After dropping the letter in the mail, Belva decided the first letter was not forceful enough. So she wrote a shorter, much more direct and less polite letter.

> Sir, —You are, or you are not, President of the National University Law School. If you are its President, I desire to say to you that I have passed through the curriculum of study in this school, and am entitled to, and demand my diploma.

> Very respectfully, Belva A. Lockwood[496]

She never heard from President Grant, but two weeks later, she received her degree from the head of the university. A week later on September 24, 1873, she was admitted to the District of Columbia bar association, only the second female to achieve this legal standing.[497]

Despite her success in becoming a practicing attorney, Belva's fight against the system was not over. She wanted to be able to take the higher paid cases, the ones tried before appeals courts and even the U.S. Supreme Court. Belva was unable, however, to get the Supreme Court

---

493 Norgren, *Equal Rights*, 52 — 53.
494 Ibid, 53.
495 Ibid, 55.
496 Ibid, 55 — 56.
497 Ibid, 56.

justices to allow her admission to the highest court in the land. The majority of justices admitted that women would not be able to practice before the U.S. Supreme Court unless Congress ordered it.[498]

Belva, accustomed to doing whatever it took to overcome the latest prejudice, went back to Congress to lobby a bill through the House and Senate. Her latest trip to Congress marked three years she had fought to obtain this legislation. The measure passed in the House, but some of the more conservative Senators feared the bill would somehow crack the door for women's suffrage.[499]

Despite these concerns, most Senators felt that women lawyers should have the same rights as male lawyers. Some legislators even suspected that male lawyers were opposed to the measure so they could more easily obtain the higher-paying cases. Senator Aaron A. Sargent, speaking in support of the measure said:

"In this land, man has ceased to dominate over his fellow," referring to the end of slavery and the granting of the vote to black men. "Let him cease to dominate over his sister."[500]

The bill was passed by the House and Senate and signed into law by President Rutherford B. Hayes. Belva's struggle with the system lasted for five years, but in the end, qualified female attorneys were eligible to practice in any federal court in the land.[501]

On March 3, 1879, Belva achieved the cherished dream of becoming the first female attorney to argue before the U.S. Supreme Court.

Many people came to see Belva practice law when she went to court. They did not come to get a glimpse of what she looked like. In fact, she was very well known throughout the city. She was a stately five feet six inches tall with dark brown hair and coal-black eyes. Rare photographs of her show a Victorian lady dressed in black velvet dresses with white ruffles at her neck and wrists. When she left her home, which doubled as a law office, she donned a pair of black gloves and blue cloth coat buttoned at the waist. Like many women of the time, she wore a variety of beads and pins. One of her favorites was a gold pendant in the form of a pair of scissors and a thimble. Another favorite was a brooch depicting the mythical god Mars driving a horse-drawn chariot.[502]

---

[498] Ibid, 61 – 62.
[499] Ibid, 62 – 63.
[500] Brown, Ibid, 37.
[501] Ibid, 63.
[502] Brown, Ibid, 31.

As a new 43-year-old attorney, she fielded a wide assortment of cases. Appropriately, in her first case as a lawyer, Belva represented a woman seeking a divorce from a cruel husband who beat her and neglected the children. Belva won the case, and the presiding judge even ordered the defendant in the action to pay Belva's fees and alimony to the plaintiff. The judge, however, expressed a doubt that the plaintiff would ever be able to collect a dime.[503] As usual, Belva was determined to get her pay.

In the 1870s, debtors in America could be sent to jail for failing to pay their debts. Belva once again went to court, this time the case was a simple debt collection. She obtained a court order demanding payment, but the defendant once again refused to pay. Belva had him locked up. Once he got a taste of prison life, he decided it was better to pay than live incarcerated.[504]

In one of Belva's most famous cases, she used the subservient station of women to obtain a not guilty verdict for her female client. The defendant had shot a police officer who forced his way into her home in search of evidence connected to a crime. She admitted shooting the officer, but her defense was that her husband had instructed her to shoot anyone attempting to force his way into their house. Because the alleged crime occurred in the District of Columbia, common law applied in the case. Under common law, women are required to obey their spouses. The defendant said she shot the officer to obey her husband, and thus, comply with the provisions of common law. A jury heard the evidence, deliberated and returned a verdict of not guilty.[505]

While Belva refused to take no for an answer and battered down doors standing in her way to become a lawyer and practice law, she was not always the serious type. The Lockport Daily Union on April 25, 1878, reported that Belva had participated in a footrace with two other female attorneys on a suburban street in Washington. As expected, the paper reported that Lockwood won the race over her competitors, Marilla M. Rucker and Lavinia Dundore. Belva would invite her fellow attorneys to share office space with her in her 20-room house on F Street.[506] Belva's daughter Lura also served as an assistant to her mother's law practice.

---

503 Ibid.
504 Ibid.
505 Ibid.
506 Brown, Ibid, 39 — 41.

While Belva's footrace may have upset some prim and proper Washingtonians, she continued to draw gasps and stares by using a big-wheeled tricycle—two large wheels opposite each other on the front and a single small wheel in the back—as transportation around the city. Onlookers worried that Belva's pedaling would cause her skirt to rise up and show her ankles or the hem of her petticoat. Belva continued to use this inexpensive and handy mode of transportation. And to avoid embarrassment to herself or others, her trike had a special dashboard that kept her skirts down.[507]

Having broken down barriers to women in education and the legal system, Belva realized women would not make significant progress until they obtained the right to vote. She and Susan B. Anthony labored to put an equal rights amendment on the national ballot for women. They attempted to gain the interest of the Republican Party in the 1880 and 1884 elections but failed to get women's suffrage on the party platform. They could not even gain the interest of a legitimate candidate. An Equal Rights party based in San Francisco nominated Belva for president, and she accepted.[508]

Some women in the women's movement, such as Susan B. Anthony and Elizabeth Cady Stanton, believed it was too early for women to run for the Presidency. They were afraid that Belva's candidacy would do more harm to the movement than help it. Belva decided to go through with it even though Anthony and Stanton opposed her.[509]

Belva was not just a token candidate. She campaigned vigorously for the office. The Equal Rights Party platform included a wide range of issues, not just women's rights matters. Some other planks in the party's platform: free education for all, pensions for disabled soldiers, an increase in wages for working men and women, and the right of Native Americans to govern themselves.[510]

Belva's campaign meetings were a circus. A woman candidate created high tension emotions. Her supporters cheered for her, and those opposed heckled loudly. Some threw vegetables. Some meetings ended in fistfights. Reporters shouted questions. Belva had to shout with all her might to be heard over the din. If not for the fact that Belva was

---

[507] Ibid.
[508] Brown, Ibid, 44.
[509] Ibid.
[510] Ibid, 46.

energized by the crowds that came to support her, she may not have had the strength to finish the campaign.[511]

When voting was over, Belva had received a little less than 5,000 votes. This number, however, does not accurately reflect her true tally. In some areas, votes for Lockwood were not counted but thrown away. Despite the disappointment, Belva—forever the optimist—was pleased with the outcome. Throughout the campaign, she noted to her supporters that she was permitted to run for President, but not allowed to vote. She said she believed her effort had "awakened the women of the country" as nothing else had done.[512]

In 1914, when Belva was 84 years old—still unable to vote—she was asked if she thought that one day a woman would be elected President. She replied:

> I look to see women in the United States senate and the house of representatives. If [a woman] demonstrates that she is fitted to be president she will some day occupy the White House. It will be entirely on her own merits, however. No movement can place her there simply because she is a woman. It will come if she proves herself mentally fit for the position.[513]

After the 1884 Presidential campaign, Belva added another important issue to her crusade—world peace. In 1885, she drafted a bill she submitted to Congress calling for an international court to preserve peace in the world. She did not evoke action by Congress, but apparently, she gained notice by the State Department, which sent her to Geneva, Switzerland, to represent the U.S. at the world's first peace conference.[514]

The Equal Rights Party in 1888 nominated Belva once again as their candidate for President. Albert H. Love, who had organized the Universal Peace Union, was her running mate. The campaign banner she carried to every event had "Peace" on one side and "Women's Rights" on the other.[515]

---

511 Ibid, 47.
512 Ibid, 50.
513 Norgren, The Woman, 142.
514 Brown, Ibid, 51.
515 Ibid, 52.

Women's rights became a common theme. In one of her speeches she asked the audience a series of rhetorical questions:

> Has God given one half of his creatures talents and gifts that are but as a mockery—wings but not to fly? Reasoning ability, but not to think, the power of poetry, but not to write? The power to sway the multitude with her eloquence but not to voice the thoughts?" She shouted the answer: "We tell you nay!"[516]

Belva did not win her second attempt at the Presidency. In fact, she did not garner as many votes the second time as she did the first. As she told her audiences in another speech:

> "I am a practical woman. If I can't get what I want, I take what I can get." Yet she admitted to a reporter, "I am very simple-minded. When I wish to do a thing, I only know one way—to keep at it till I get it."[517]

These characteristics would serve Belva well as she took on one of the greatest legal fights of her career, one that lasted 30 years and resulted in a $5 million judgment, the largest in American history at that time.

Belva's landmark case dated back to 1838 when the United States government attempted to force all the Cherokee living in western North Carolina to move to a reservation in Oklahoma. Some 14,000 Cherokee were force marched west through bitter winter weather so severe that 4,000 died along the way. This tragic journey of death and despair is known in American history as the "Trail of Tears." More than a thousand Cherokee hid from soldiers in the North Carolina Smoky Mountains and did not make that fateful journey.[518]

While the federal government traded the Cherokee their original land for land in Oklahoma, the Native American tribe was to be awarded a $1 million payment. It had not occurred, and members of the tribe

---

[516] Ibid, 52.
[517] Ibid, 53.
[518] Ibid.

wanted their money plus interest. Belva knew that the interest on a million dollars would take the potential award to well over the initial agreement figure. She also knew that the case would involve three or four thousand families totaling 12 to 15 thousand people. It would require massive research on her part, as well as travel to the distant Cherokee nations to conduct interviews.[519]

Unfortunately for Belva and the rest of her family, tragedy struck suddenly again—in 1894, Lura died unexpectedly. Belva was heartbroken. Lura's death meant that Belva had lost her daughter, business partner and co-worker. Belva agreed to help Lura's husband take care of their four-year-old son, DeForest. In only six years, however, DeForest's father also died. Belva took over full childcare.[520]

Once again, as she had done so often in the past, Belva concentrated on her work to relieve her sadness and grief. She kept pursuing the women's rights issue. While she was not successful in her efforts at women's suffrage, she joined with other women to draft a bill that made a number of positive changes for American women. The bill provided a fair inheritance law for married women; granted them the right to sue, buy and sell property, enter into contracts and to conduct other aspects of their personal business. Even more importantly, the bill prevented a married man from throwing his wife out and keeping the children— unless he could prove she was an unfit mother. President William McKinley signed the bill into law on June 1, 1896.[521]

Next, Belva threw her energies into the Cherokee nation case. Her first involvement occurred in 1875 when she met James Taylor, a Cherokee who had been representing the tribe in Washington. She assisted Taylor in writing a memorandum to the Commissioner of Indian Affairs outlining the grievances under which the Cherokee had suffered over many decades. She essentially represented the Eastern Cherokee, the ones who had refused to move west and remained in the North Carolina mountains.[522]

Over the years, however, Taylor fell from favor within the Eastern Cherokee tribe. The new leader, Nimrod Smith, signed an agreement with another law firm, and they filed a motion to end Belva's

---

519 Ibid, 54.
520 Ibid.
521 Ibid, 55.
522 Norgren, *Belva Lockwood: The Woman*, 206 — 207.

representation of the tribe. The Chief Justice Charles Drake removed Belva from the case. The tribes new legal team argued the case using a different legal approach and lost.[523]

While it appeared that Belva had lost all legal claim to the case, she did not let despair get the best of her. Once again she remained optimistic and stayed in touch with Taylor, who moved to the Cherokee West nation, made friends there and re-established his standing with the Eastern group. Now, with Taylor as a legitimate representative of at least a major part of the tribe, Belva had the proper authorization from Taylor to re-enter the case. Looking for a new legal angle, she noted that there was a new government deal with the Cherokee, which called for a complete accounting of all monies due the tribe in treaties going back to 1817. Government accountants prepared a report for Congress stating that the federal government owed the Cherokee several million dollars.[524]

Belva's optimism was beginning to pay off. She and Taylor saw this latest development as an opportunity to get back into the fight. Belva still had not received appropriate authorization through a recognized chief or tribal council. Another attorney, Robert Owen, had. Nevertheless, Belva had represented members of the tribe for two decades and represented the Cherokee who were members of Taylor's faction. On September 13, 1901, she successfully tapped into Owen's case by filing a motion to intervene on behalf of Taylor and his friends. Her authorization came from a thousand Cherokee who had given her power of attorney. She added another 4,000 clients by subcontracting powers of attorney from other local lawyers. At this point, there were three major groups involved in the lawsuit: the Cherokee represented by Belva, the tribal members represented by Owen, and the Cherokee Nation West, which continued to claim the award as their own.[525]

The Court of Claims, a federal court whose responsibility was to settle claims against the U.S. government, heard the case on March 24, 1902. Several weeks later they issued a decision: they had no opinion as to whether or not the claims should be paid. Now the case was back in the hands of Congress. After some delay, legislators instructed the lawyers for the plaintiffs to file a formal lawsuit in the Court of Claims.

---

523 Ibid.
524 Ibid.
525 Ibid.

This action would require a full judicial ruling as opposed to a finding of fact, as was done in the first action before the Court of Claims.[526]

This time Belva and Owen filed a lawsuit on behalf of the Eastern and Western Cherokee on March 10, 1903. The case was argued in February 1905. This time the Cherokee won. Chief Justice Charles Nott ruled that both factions—East and West— deserved an equal share. Belva, 75 years old, was elated by the victory and the possibility of receiving a fee of as much as $50,000. But her work was not yet over. The government filed an appeal with the U.S. Supreme Court.[527]

The court began hearing the appeal on January 16, 1906. Three months later the court ruled on the claims of the Cherokee plaintiffs. The court affirmed the million dollar award for the plaintiffs, but reversed the lower court decision that the Cherokee West group should share in the judgment.[528]

Even though Belva had looked forward eagerly to receive her anticipated large fee, Owen stopped the court from setting aside Belva's fee before the judgment was distributed. Owen used the tactic of forcing Belva to collect her fee from each of the individual Cherokee she represented. Once again, Belva refused to accept defeat and hired an attorney to represent her in what was becoming a vicious fight for a total of three-quarter's of a million dollars in attorney fees.[529]

Belva learned all the other attorneys had organized against her and were attempting to cut her out of the judgment. They claimed she had lacked proper power of attorney from any tribal entity involved in the lawsuit and that she only represented a group of individual families who employed her services. They argued, therefore, that she should collect her fee from the people she represented.[530]

The hearing judge agreed with the lawyers who sided against Belva. He decreed that all attorneys, except Belva, should share in a 15 percent award. She appealed the decision through her attorney and a compromise was offered: she would receive $18,000—not $50,000 as she had expected—from the attorney fee fund and collect additional fees from her individual clients at the rate of 10 percent, not 15 percent.[531]

---

526 Ibid, 208.
527 Ibid, 209.
528 Ibid, 210.
529 Ibid, 211.
530 Ibid, 212 – 213.
531 Ibid, 213.

By her own admission, the judgment was a bitter disappointment and stinging blow to her ego and finances. She claimed she had mortgaged her house to continue pressing the case and also owed her own attorney $3,000 in fees. She sent James Taylor, her original client in the Cherokee matters, now "old and feeble," a thousand dollars. Taylor died shortly after the two visited in November 1906.[532]

Now 77 years old, Belva began to think about her legacy. She wanted her old alma mater, which had become part of Syracuse University, to recognize her accomplishments. She asked Syracuse University dean, Frank Smalley, to award her an honorary doctor of laws degree. While she did not receive an immediate response, eventually she received the honor.[533]

In 1912, Belva became a member of the new American Woman's Republic. A brainchild of St. Louis publisher Edward Gardner Lewis, his vision called for creating a second republic in America with a President, Vice President and other leaders. The two republics would exist side by side until women won suffrage. At that point the two republics would merge into one. Although Belva ran for President as organizing began, she did not win the top position. She agreed to serve, however, as the republic's attorney general.[534]

By the time Belva had reached 85 years old, the results of a lifetime of work to secure women's rights were obvious: women could vote in 12 states and the territory of Alaska. Forever the optimist, Belva gave a speech on her 85th birthday, October 15, 1915, in which she made the bold statement: "Suffrage is no longer an issue. It is an accomplished fact. Those states which have denied it to women will come around."[535]

Indeed, Belva was proved correct. By June 4, 1919, the U.S. House and Senate had approved the 19th Amendment to the Constitution giving women the right to vote. The amendment was passed on to the states to ratify. The required three-fourths approval was secured when Tennessee became the 36th state to ratify the amendment out of the existing 48 states. The Tennessee governor notified the U.S. Secretary of State that the amendment had been ratified. On August 26, 1920, the

---

[532] Ibid, 213.
[533] Ibid, 217.
[534] Ibid, 220.
[535] Brown, Ibid, 57.

19th Amendment was law, and women were allowed to vote that fall in the Presidential election.

Unfortunately, Belva did not live to see the accomplishment of the event she worked so hard for. She died May 20, 1917, almost three years before women were finally granted the right to vote.

Of all the women at the 1848 Seneca Falls meeting in which women's rights became a national issue, only one was still living in 1920: Charlotte Woodward. Sadly, it is believed that Woodward, who was a 19-year-old glove maker in 1848, never got an opportunity to vote. She was too ill and feeble to leave the house.[536]

No one individual in American history accomplished so much for all women in this country as did Belva Lockwood. She did it by developing her talents, intelligence and ability fully, attacking anything standing in her way. Her optimism and belief in herself seemed to accomplish miracles. With a limited education, she became a teacher at 14. She acquired a higher education so she could become a better teacher, despite the fact that women were discouraged from attending college. As a single mother, she realized she needed a good profession to ensure strong earning power. She entered law school and graduated, but she was forced to go to President Grant to make the school give her the degree she had earned. And when the U.S. Supreme Court would not admit her to the bar, she helped lobby a bill through Congress that opened the door for women lawyers to practice in the highest court in the land.

Even though Belva gained admittance to the Supreme Court in 1879, it would be just over a hundred years later—1981—that Sandra Day O'Connor would become the nation's first female Supreme Court justice. And it would be another 25 years before Ruth Bader Ginsburg joined the court as only the second female justice in the court's history.

While women's suffrage was important to Belva, she had a profound concern for many issues affecting American politics and culture. She called for protection of public lands and reform for family law and supported a tariff whose proceeds would be used to help war veterans. Even though Belva could not vote for President at the time, she

536 Judith Wellman, "Charlotte Woodward," Women's Rights, National Park Service, U.S. Department of the Interior, www.nps.gov/wori/historyculture/charlotte-woodward.htm, accessed April 12, 2010.

discovered she could not be prevented from running. And she did so, albeit unsuccessfully, on two occasions.

Finally, her determination and optimism led to a great victory for the Cherokee Indians seeking compensation for lands taken by the federal government. The $5 million award was the largest in history at that time.

Never one to rest on her laurels, Belva was constantly on the attack to oppose any forces or policies that put a limit to the expansion of the human imagination and soul. She was as involved in the international peace movement as she was women's issues. Her activism transcended more than a moral or ethical imperative. She knocked down legal and cultural barriers as a single mother who wanted to provide the best for her family.

She made a breach in the centuries old social walls that devalued and demeaned women. She invited her sisters, present and future, to crash through with her. They did so in overwhelming numbers, and the United States and world have been the benefactors of a vast new wave of talent, intelligence and optimism that has changed the world.

# KING DAVID

The story of David and Goliath is perhaps one of the most recounted episodes of the Bible, illustrating the power of good over evil, hope over despair and courage over fear. The plot is simple: a young shepherd boy, armed with smooth stones, a primitive sling and a belief in God's protective powers over his chosen people, defeats the fearsome giant Goliath. Then David adds the *coup de grace* — he beheads Goliath using the giant's own sword. This incident stands out vividly in the history of Western civilization as an exciting example of the power of optimism to inspire an individual to achieve the seemingly impossible.

Often when coaching high school athletics and preparing my team for a game, I would read the words of 1 Samuel 17 and watch as their eyes became larger and their confidence level would swell as they prepared to meet their challenge.

But focusing on a single incident in the life of Israel's greatest king does not depict adequately the hardships and challenges David overcame in becoming one of the most important leaders portrayed in the Old Testament. He was born into poverty and repeatedly beset with hardships. Yet he refused to bend to these burdens. Instead, he wrapped himself in a cloak of optimism that would help him weather the storms of his life and times, outshine every Israelite warrior and slay the terrifying Philistine giant Goliath.

Later, David became a great military leader, leading his army into battle, soundly defeating the Philistines and uniting the two Hebrew kingdoms of Judah and Israel under one dominant kingdom. Biblical scholars and historians are quick to note, however, that as awesome as David's leadership abilities were, some of his actions seemed confusing and contradictory, and raised questions about his morality and integrity. Overlooking his human shortcomings, however, David's contribution to Jewish history and tradition is undeniable. Sitting as only the second king of Israel, he was also a talented musician and poet. He is credited with composing 73 of the 150 psalms or Biblical hymns contained in the Book of Psalms, including the oft-quoted 23rd Psalm.

David's unexpected ascendance began with a defiance of God — though not on his part. Traditionally, God has supported those who followed His commands and punished those who disobeyed. In the first book of Samuel, God clearly ordered the Hebrews' first king, Saul, to kill every man, woman and child of the Amalekites, a traditional enemy of Israel, and to do the same with all of the captured livestock (1 Samuel 15). However, Saul disobeyed. He ordered everyone killed but saved the life of the Amalekite king Agag. Saul also allowed his troops to keep all the best cattle and sheep. When Samuel confronted him, Saul gave the excuse that he was going to use the captured livestock as a sacrifice to God.

> But Samuel replied, "What is more pleasing to the Lord: your burnt offerings and sacrifices or your obedience to his voice? Obedience is far better than sacrifice. Listening to him is much better than offering the fat of rams. Rebellion is as bad as the sin of witchcraft, and stubbornness is as bad as worshipping idols. So because you have rejected the word of the Lord, he has rejected you from being king."[537]

Saul realized his mistake, admitted his sins and begged for forgiveness. Samuel replied: "And he who is the Glory of Israel will not lie, nor will he change his mind, for he is not human that he should change his mind." (1 Samuel 15:29)

Consequently, Saul fell out of favor with God, and God sought to replace him with His handpicked successor: David. The fact that God chose David is a strong argument for the power of optimism. David was the slightest of the seven sons of his father Jesse. How could he expect to be anointed king? Besides, traditionally the older sons in a family are bestowed with such honor before the younger. David's chances seemed minute.

Once God decided to replace Saul, however, Samuel was instructed to secretly anoint David as king (1 Samuel 16:13). But despite God's favor, David's path to glory would be rough and shaky. God did not magically remove Saul from power and install David as his new leader of the Israelites. Instead, David relied on patience, tenacity and a belief in

---

[537] 1 Samuel 15: 22 — 23. Unless otherwise noted, all scripture notations are taken from The Holy Bible, New Living Translation, copyright 1996. Used by permission of Tyndale House Publishers Inc., Wheaton, Illinois, 60189. All rights reserved.

the goodness of God and a trust in His promises. These qualities — patience, trust and steadfastness — are powerful traits of the optimist.

They would serve David well, too. His human desires, cruelty in battle and weakness in the face of temptation nearly brought him down. But miraculously, God did not abandon David or allow him to fall out of favor. Throughout the three main periods of David's life — simple shepherd, ruthless mercenary, great ruler (and, consistently, a common sinner) — God stood by him. And David optimistically believed that He always would.

David's journey from shepherd boy to ruler of the united kingdoms of Israel and Judah began after God removed favor from Saul and brought upon the king a mental distress described in scripture as a "tormenting spirit that filled him with depression and fear." (1 Samuel 16:14) Some in Saul's court suggested the king try music therapy. "Let us find a good musician to play the harp for you whenever the tormenting spirit is bothering you. The harp music will quiet you, and you will soon be well again" (1 Samuel 16:16). At the suggestion of his advisors, Saul sent for David, known throughout the land as an accomplished harpist. David's music soothed Saul and enabled him to gain admission into the king's court.

The physical threat of the giant Goliath, however, thrust David into the military limelight. Goliath, a Philistine soldier eight- to 10-feet tall by various accounts, issued an insulting challenge to the Israelites: Send one of their warriors to fight him one-on-one or lose many lives in army-to-army combat. (1 Samuel 17) Goliath's size and ferocity frightened the soldiers. No one was willing to respond to his taunts and challenges. Finally, David told Saul he would fight the giant.

Saul tried to warn him off, reminding David he was only a young man while Goliath was a seasoned warrior. But David did not dwell on the severity of the challenge. He told Saul that as a shepherd, he had used only a wooden club to protect his flock from lions and bears. Saul tried to equip him with the king's own armor — a helmet and coat of mail — but after trying it on, David decided to forego the protection. It did not feel right. He was not used to it. (1 Samuel 17:38 — 39)

Ultimately, David relied not on heavy armor or sophisticated weapons to defeat the fearsome giant. He relied entirely on his cunning, speed and agility — and the optimistic belief that they would all work to his eventual advantage. As the battle began, David rushed forward and launched a smooth stone into Goliath's forehead. The giant crashed to the ground face forward like a huge felled tree. Then, with no sword of his own, David grabbed the downed giant's own saber and beheaded him. (1 Samuel 17:51).

The Israelites hailed David as a conquering hero, a celebrity status that provided an opportunity to meet Saul's son Jonathan, with whom he became a lifelong friend. Unfortunately, this adulation evoked only jealousy from Saul. While Israelites cheered for Saul, they also cheered for David in a chant that kindled Saul's hatred of Goliath's slayer: "Saul has killed his thousands, and David his tens of thousands!" (1 Samuel 18:7) One day in a fit of anger, Saul tried to pin David's body to the wall by hurling a spear at him. David dodged it and escaped, but Saul banned David from his presence. However, David did not retire from public life. He continued to prosper in struggles against the Philistines, exhibiting an optimism and confidence that carried him far in battle. His popularity continued to grow.

Eventually, Saul sent David into combat to win one of his daughters as a bride. In reality, he was hoping the enemy would kill the young man. (1 Samuel 18:17). Instead, David performed well and won the hand and heart of the king's daughter Michal. "When the king realized how much the Lord was with David and how much Michal loved him, he became even more afraid of him, and he remained David's enemy for the rest of his life." (1 Samuel 18:28 – 29)

Saul then invoked Jonathan and his followers to kill David. Because they were so close, Jonathan warned David of the plot to kill him, and he spoke to his father on David's behalf. Saul welcomed David back into the palace as before. Before long, however, the "tormenting spirit" struck Saul again and, in his agony, he hurled another spear at David as he was playing his harp for the disturbed monarch. (1 Samuel 19:10). David fled into the wilderness, taking up residence in a cave with friends and family, joined by a number of Saul's subjects who were discontent with the king. Soon, David had assembled a force of about 400 men. (1 Samuel 22:2).

While Saul had made at least two attempts to kill him, David spared Saul's life on two occasions. Despite the king's hatred, David's optimism negated any fear that the king would eventually succeed in killing him. In a face-to-face meeting, David asked Saul what he had done to deserve death. Saul admitted he had sinned against David. "Then Saul confessed, 'I have sinned. Come back home, my son, and I will no longer try to harm you, for you have valued my life today. I have been a fool and very, very wrong.'" (1 Samuel 26:21)

David, however, correctly calculated that Saul would continue his vendetta. As an added precaution, he took refuge with the Israelites' bitter enemy, the Philistines. The fact that David would side with Israel's traditional enemy reveals his will to survive at all costs. It also demonstrated that David did not fear the Philistines any more than he feared Saul. David and his followers traveled to Gath — one of the five Philistine city-states — and came under the protection of King Achish.

Although he had joined the Philistines, David created an illusion to King Achish that he was fighting the Israelites. David and his force raided the Geshurites, the Girzites and the Amalekites, traditional enemies of Israel. With each raid, David left no witnesses, killing every man, woman and child. He also seized all their property and livestock. When King Achish asked David which villages he had attacked, David falsely reported that he had been in the south of Judah fighting the Jerahmeelites and the Kenites, two tribes friendly to the Israelites. Because David had slaughtered all of his victims, his lies worked. No one was alive to contradict his story. (1 Samuel 27:11).

King Achish believed that by attacking the Jerahmeelites and the Kenites, David had permanently severed his ties with the Israelites. The king was so confident of David's loyalty that he asked him to become part of an army preparing to attack the Israelites. David agreed. But other Philistine princes objected, fearing David would show his true colors and turn on them in the heat of battle. (1 Samuel 29:1 — 11,)

The Philistines departed to attack the Israelites in Jezreel, and David and his troops returned to Ziklag, where they had been staying while under King Achish's protection. When they arrived, however, they discovered that the Amalekites had attacked their village, burned and plundered it and carried off all the women and children. David and his followers wept openly at what they found. Some were so bitter and angry about losing their wives and children that they talked about stoning David.

Despite his grief and anguish, David refused to accept defeat. He did not resign himself to fate by believing there was no use in attempting to rescue the hostages, instead urging his followers to pursue and overtake the Amalekites and to recover their women and children. Once again, he relied upon unrelenting optimism to carry the day, refusing to cut his losses or surrender to fear of defeat or death. He and 400 of his 600-member army pursued the Amalekites, convinced they would find and triumph over the enemy.

Almost miraculously, David and his followers found a young Egyptian slave, abandoned by his Amalekite master, wandering aimlessly in the desert. David asked the Egyptian to lead him to the band of Amalekites, and the slave agreed. David and his forces found their enemies celebrating, unsuspecting of any looming danger. The Israelites attacked before dawn, and fighting continued until the following evening. David and his troops recovered the stolen property along with the hostages, including his own two wives. (1 Samuel 30:18 — 20)

While David was successful in his combat, King Saul was not as fortunate. The Philistine force killed Saul and his three sons, including David's beloved friend Jonathan. Critically wounded, Saul implored his armor bearer to end his life in an act of mercy. The servant refused. Saul then fell on his own sword, ending his suffering. Later, a young Amalekite sought out David to report that he had killed Saul in accordance with Saul's pleas for a merciful death. David condemned the youth for killing one of God's anointed and ordered the Amalekite executed on the spot.

With Saul's death, the question arose as to who would become Israel's second king. David was a popular candidate, but the ruling power was split: Saul's son Isbosheth became king of the northern kingdom of Israel; David became ruler of Judah, the southern kingdom of the Hebrews. The two kingdoms were at war for two years. Hostilities ended after two assassins killed Ishbosheth as he took a mid-day nap. The killers removed the king's head and rushed to David to show him they had avenged Saul's attempts to kill David. David surprised the two by reacting in an unexpected way, saying:

> As surely as the Lord lives, the one who saves me from my enemies, I will tell you the truth. Once before someone told me "Saul is dead," thinking he was bringing me good news. But I seized him and killed him at Ziklag. That's the reward I gave him for his news! Now what reward should I give the wicked men

who have killed an innocent man in his own house
and on his own bed? Should I not also demand your
very lives? (2 Samuel 4:9 — 11)

As he had done with the man who said he had killed Saul, David ordered
the immediate deaths of Ishbosheth's two murderers.

David made history by assuming the leadership of Israel and Judah
at only 30 years of age. For the first time, the two kingdoms were united
under a single House of David. David's great optimism and trust in his
Lord was at last paying off. He defeated the Jebusites, who inhabited
Jerusalem, and made the "City of David" the capital of a united Israel.
When the Philistines heard David was king, they united against him.
David asked God if his enemies would be "delivered up into (his) hand."
After God assured David that he would prevail, the young warrior-king
attacked and defeated the Philistines. (2 Samuel 5:19) David's over-
brimming optimism had filled him with the confidence to win. Shortly
afterward, the Philistines regrouped and attacked David in force a
second time. Once again, after asking if the Philistines would be
delivered to him and receiving God's assurances, David defeated the
Philistines and drove them from Israel's territory.

As a final demonstration of how David's power and optimism would
put Israel in a position of strength and leadership, he recovered the
Jews' sacred Ark of the Covenant, which the Philistines had captured.
David ordered that his followers take the Ark to Jerusalem, which then
became the capital of Israel. (2 Samuel 6:1 – 5) Even though the Ark had
always been housed in a tent, David contemplated building a great
sanctuary of wood to accommodate the Ark in a permanent home in
Jerusalem. The prophet Nathan encouraged him to do it. But one night
Nathan had a dream in which God spoke to him. God told Nathan that
Israel now had a permanent home free from its enemies and granted a
new covenant promise that He would create a house of kings for David,
not a physical house of wood. God instructed Nathan to tell David that
the next king of Israel would build the temple for the Ark. God promised
that the House of David would be secure forever. (2 Samuel 7:11 – 17)
God also pledged to treat David's descendants as sons:

I will be his father, and he will be my son. If he sins, I
will use other nations to punish him. But my unfailing

love will not be taken from him as I took it from Saul, whom I removed before you. Your dynasty and your kingdom will continue for all time before me, and your throne will be secure forever. (2 Samuel 7:14 – 16)

At this point in David's life, everything seemed to be going his way. He continued to accumulate one military victory after another. He conquered Gath, the Philistines largest city. He defeated the land of Moab. He destroyed the army of Hadadezer, son of Rehob, king of Zobah. He killed 22,000 Arameans from Damascus who attempted to help Hadadezer's forces. He killed 18,000 Edomites. He defeated the Ammonites, killing 700 charioteers and 40,000 horsemen.

As David rode the crest of his military success, however, trouble was already brewing. He sent an army commanded by his nephew Joab to lay siege to the Philistine city of Rabbah. While his army was away, David spied a comely young woman, Bathsheba, bathing on a rooftop. Unaware at that time Bathsheba was married, the king was smitten. He directed an aide to find out her identity and then invite her to his palace. During her palace visit, they slept together. Later she sent word that she was pregnant with his child.

Rather than face the consequences, David immediately schemed to cover up his actions. He sent for Bathsheba's husband, Uriah the Hittite, a member of David's armed forces. His plan was for Bathsheba to sleep with her husband, and then, the king reasoned, everyone would assume the father of the baby to be Uriah. But David's scheme failed when Uriah refused to feast or sleep with his wife while his comrades were suffering the deprivations of the battlefield. So David decided he must implement another, more diabolical plan. He ordered his military commander to put Uriah in harm's way and then pull back all forces so that the enemy would kill Uriah in battle. David's orders were executed. Uriah died. David married the widow Bathsheba.

The book of 2 Samuel states that God was "very displeased" with David and sent Nathan the prophet to tell David a parable that would illustrate what he had done. The parable involved a rich man who took a lamb from a poor man and slaughtered it to feed a guest. David was incensed at the actions of the rich man and said, "As surely as the Lord lives, any man who would do such a thing deserves to die!" (2 Samuel

12:5) Nathan revealed to David that the parable was about his actions to steal Bathsheba from Uriah, and delivered a message from God: "From this time on, the sword will be a constant threat to your family, because you have despised me by taking Uriah's wife to be your own."(2 Samuel 12:10). God also told David through Nathan:

> Because of what you have done, I, the Lord will cause your own household to rebel against you. I will give your wives to another man, and he will go to bed with them in public view. You did it secretly, but I will do this to you openly in the sight of all Israel. (2 Samuel 12:11 – 12)

David realized his guilt and confessed his sins to Nathan. But the prophet told him that God would not take his life for this sin, but David would pay in another way: the child born of the illicit union would die. Just as Nathan predicted, the baby became "deathly ill." But David would not give up, optimistically believing he could change God's mind. A distraught David begged God to spare the child, but his actions were to no avail. The child died.

When his advisors notified David of the death, he did the most curious thing from their point of view. He rose, bathed, changed his clothes and went to the Tabernacle to worship God. Then he returned to the palace and ate. The advisors questioned David as to why he was grief-stricken, while the child was alive, but stopped mourning after the boy had died. David's response is revealing about his ability to deal with death, to accept his fate and to get on with life:

> I fasted and wept while the child was alive, for I said, "Perhaps the Lord will be gracious to me and let the child live." But why should I fast when he is dead? Can I bring him back again? I will go to him one day, but he cannot return to me. (2 Samuel 12:22 – 23)

It is also important to note that David did not agonize over the past, beating himself up for what he should have done. Nor did he project future misfortune based on what had happened. He accepted God's judgment as final.

In the end, David's optimism proved correct. He slept with Bathsheba, and she became pregnant again. She produced another child who was to become Solomon, the proverbial wisest king of all time in Israel. Solomon also received the privilege of building the Temple and ruling over Israel during the nation's golden age. Tragedy became triumph, due in no small part to David's willingness to simply move forward, optimistic and confident in his relationship with God.

Still, his family troubles were far from over. David's son Absalom had a sister, Tamar, who became the object of adoration by her half-brother Amnon. Amnon was so obsessed that he was unable to control his desire. In his crazed lust, Amnon raped the girl after tricking her into being alone with him, leaving Tamar shamed in the eyes of the nation. But Absalom took no action for two years. Then he prepared a feast for all of David's sons and invited Amnon. Absalom conspired with his servants to get Amnon intoxicated and then kill him. At Absalom's signal, his servants did so. The other brothers fled in terror.

Absalom also took flight in fear of the king's retribution. Though Absalom and David were eventually reunited, Absalom began planning a rebellion by first winning the hearts and minds of David's subjects. He eventually gathered enough popular support to march on Jerusalem, forcing David and his followers to escape from the City of David. The king left behind 10 concubines to keep the palace in order. As David and his family fled, the king got a taste of the enmity his enemies felt for him. Shimei, a relative of the deceased King Saul, cursed David:

> Get out of here, you murderer, you scoundrel! The Lord is paying you back for murdering Saul and his family. You stole his throne, and now the Lord has given it to your son Absalom. At last you will taste some of your own medicine, you murderer! (2 Samuel 16:7 – 8)

These curses angered David's advisors, and they wanted to kill Shimei. But David, well aware of God's intention to punish him through others, patiently accepted the unpleasantness and responded:

> If the Lord has told him to curse me, who am I to stop him? My own son is trying to kill me. Shouldn't this

relative of Saul have even more reason to do so? Leave
him alone and let him curse, for the Lord has told him
to do it.

Ever the optimist, David concluded: "And perhaps the Lord will see that
I am being wronged and will bless me because of these curses."

But David was to suffer even more at the hands of Absalom. An
advisor of David's, Ahithophel, turned on the king and joined Absalom
in Jerusalem. One of his first pieces of advice helped fulfill a prophecy
God made to David: another man would sleep with David's wives in
plain view. Ahithophel advised Absalom to sleep with the 10 concubines
David had left at the palace, saying:

> "Go and sleep with your father's concubines, for he
> has left them here to keep the house. Then all Israel
> will know that you have insulted him beyond hope of
> reconciliation, and they will give you their support."
> So they set up a tent on the palace roof where
> everyone could see it, and Absalom went into the tent
> to sleep with his father's concubines.
>
> Absalom followed Athithophel's advice, just as David
> had done. For every word Athithophel spoke seemed
> as wise as though it had come directly from the mouth
> of God. (2 Samuel 16:21 – 23)

Another of David's advisors, Hushai, remained in Jerusalem and
pretended to be on Absalom's side. But his true purpose was to thwart
Absalom's efforts to kill David and secure his rule. When Ahithophel
advised Absalom to take 12,000 warriors and immediately pursue
David, Hushai recommended instead that Absalom gather as many of
Israel's forces as possible before engaging the king in combat. Hushai
also sent word to David to escape as quickly as possible into the
wilderness beyond the Jordan River. (2 Samuel 17:15 – 16)

There, David's forces regrouped and attacked Absalom's army.
Some of the fighting occurred in the thick forest of Ephraim. Twenty
thousand men died in the fierce combat. Absalom attempted to flee
David's forces, but his hair got tangled in the branches of a tree. His

mount rode out from under him, leaving Absalom dangling helplessly by his hair in a tree. Even though David had ordered before the fighting began that Absalom was not to be killed, the king's commander Joab stabbed Absalom to death as he hung from the branches. (2 Samuel 18:6 – 17) Learning of the death, David was grief-stricken and wept for Absalom. Joab went to the king's chambers and rebuked him for acting in such a manner:

> We saved your life today and the lives of your sons, your daughters, your wives and concubines. Yet you act like this, making us feel ashamed as though we had done something wrong. You seem to love those who hate you and hate those who love you. You have made it clear today that we mean nothing to you. If Absalom had lived and all of us had died, you would be pleased. Now go out there and congratulate the troops, for I swear by the Lord that if you don't, not a single one of them will remain here tonight. Then you will be worse off than you have ever been. (2 Samuel 19:5 – 7)

David complied, and went into the city where his subjects warmly greeted him.

He also sent priests to the leaders of Judah to ask why they had not yet accepted him as their king. Additionally, he communicated that he intended to replace Joab with Amasa, David's nephew, who had sided with Absalom and commanded his troops against David. Upon learning this, Amasa convinced the leaders of Judah to welcome David back to the throne. (2 Samuel 19:11 – 14) David's optimism led him to show mercy to former enemies such as Amasa.

Others benefited from David's optimism and charity as well. When David crossed the Jordan River, the citizens of Judah rushed to the river to greet him. Among them was Shimei, who had cursed David so vilely as the king was fleeing Jerusalem. Shimei fell prostrate at David's feet, apologized and begged for forgiveness. One of David's nephews, Abishai, the son of David's sister Zeruiah, said Shimei should die for cursing God's anointed king. "What am I going to do with you sons of Zeruiah!" David exclaimed. "This is not a day for execution but for celebration! I am once again the king of Israel." Then turning to Shimei, David vowed, "Your life will be spared." (2 Samuel 19:21 – 23)

Despite the appearance of peace and prosperity, jealousy once again began to divide the kingdoms of Israel and Judah. Because David had come from Judah, the men of Judah had taken the lead in helping the king cross the Jordan to return to Jerusalem. The 10 other tribes of Israel complained they had not been given an opportunity to help. (2 Samuel 19:41 – 43) The argument grew more and more heated until, finally, a "troublemaker" named Sheba from the tribe of Benjamin blew a trumpet and shouted: "We have nothing to do with David. We want no part of this son of Jesse. Come on, you men of Israel, let's all go home!" (2 Samuel 20:1)

To deal with this rebellion, David asked Amasa to mobilize the men of Judah and report back to him in three days. When Amasa was unable to do so within that time frame, David told his nephew Abishai to take the king's troops and capture Sheba before the troublemaker took refuge in a fortified city. Abishai joined forces with Joab, who was leading his own army, and they met Amasa and his forces en route to a battle with Sheba. Joab greeted Amasa warmly. But as Amasa reached out to touch him, Joab stabbed him to death with a dagger he had concealed in his hand. Through murder, Joab had recovered leadership of David's combined forces. (2 Samuel 20:7 – 10)

Sheba took shelter in the fortified city of Abel-beth-maccah, and David's forces prepared to lay siege. Just as the battering of the town's walls began, a woman resident of the town asked Joab if there was any way to prevent the destruction of the city. Joab replied that if the city residents turned Sheba over to him he would spare the city. The woman promised to throw Sheba's head over the stone wall. She went to the city's residents and told them about the agreement with Joab. They cut off Sheba's head and threw it over the wall to Joab, who called back his troops. The city was saved from destruction, and the rebellion was over.

Eventually David grew old and infirm. Adonijah, his son by wife Haggith, decided to become king on his own initiative. Nathan the prophet told Bathsheba about Adonijah's action. Both she and David wanted their son Solomon to succeed him as ruler. When David learned what was going on, he ordered Solomon anointed as king. (1 King 1: 1 – 35) In his last words to Solomon, David advised his son always to obey God:

Observe the requirements of the Lord your God and
follow all his ways. Keep each of the laws, commands,
regulations, and stipulations written in the laws of
Moses so that you will be successful in all you do and
wherever you go. If you do this, then the Lord will
keep the promise he made to me: "If your descendants
live as they should and follow me faithfully with all
their heart and soul, one of them will always sit on the
throne of Israel." (1 Kings 2:3 – 4)

According to prophetic writings of the Bible and ancient rabbinic
writings on Jewish law and tradition, the messiah would be either a
direct descendant of David or David himself, raised from the dead. [538]
Thus, David has for centuries served as the ultimate symbol of optimism
for the Jewish people. The concept of the coming of Christ, the
"anointed one," may be considered an optimistic outlook for the future
of humankind.

David also represents a turning point in the history of God's
relationship with his chosen. For a king such as Saul, displeasing God
was a colossal blunder. There was no way in which Saul was able to
overcome his transgressions and receive forgiveness. David, on the other
hand, was continuously breaking God's commandments. Yet David
never broke faith with God, and — quite optimistically — continued to
serve Him. And God was forgiving. While He punished David severely
for his sins, God never totally abandoned him. David never waivered
from his determination to serve God.

David's positive outlook enabled him to become the greatest ruler in
Israel's history. And each time he suffered personal setbacks, his
optimism and persistence kept him going. His spirit seemed to imprint
itself on an entire nation of Jews who survived hundreds of years of
prejudice and persecution. Without an optimistic belief in the ultimate
triumph of Judaism over evil, the state of Israel might not exist today. It
is truly a stirring example of what can be accomplished — and how
much can be endured — with an optimistic view of the world. . . and of
life itself.

---

[538] Jonathan Kirsch. *King David: The Real Life of the Man Who Ruled Israel*,
(Ballentine Books: New York, NY, 2000.), 289.

# LARRY DOBY

History's firsts are quickly identifiable. They are stories of individuals who overcame unprecedented challenges, and we easily draw upon their names to reference the greatest achievers of our time. But what credit do we give the second man on the moon, the second to fly or— in the case of Lawrence Eugene "Larry" Doby — the second black American to play major league baseball?

Too often, society seems to relegate "second-place finishers" to a historical footnote, even though they may have defied the same odds and pushed equally as hard as their counterpart "firsts." For those of us from Camden, South Carolina, Larry Doby is a "first" and a hero.

There is another story behind those who followed others, because many did so with little or no support or tribute. As such, they should be remembered as some of the greatest individuals of their time and ours, because they confronted challenges that can only be taken on by the most hopeful, passionate and optimistic individuals. For they, too, are heroes, and their experiences provide each of us lessons of great value and inspiration.

On April 15, 1947, Jackie Robinson made history when he became the first African-American to play baseball for a major league team, the Brooklyn Dodgers.[539] He did this during the height of racial segregation in America and during a time when the issue of allowing blacks to play in major league baseball was extremely contentious. Baseball commissioners fought pressure from both sides of the controversy for years. Some team owners openly spoke of their angst over allowing blacks to play in "their" league while others were too afraid to take any initiative for fear of ridicule from colleagues. Major leaguers abided by what Leo Durocher, then manager of the Dodgers, called the "grapevine understanding or subterranean rule," which barred blacks from the majors.[540] Meanwhile, black Americans were fighting their own war on segregation on the various social and political battlegrounds and would continue to do so through much of the century.

---

539 Larry Moffi and Jonathan Kronstadt. *Crossing the Line: Black Major Leaguers, 1947 – 1959*, (Jefferson, N.C.: McFarland Company, Inc., 1994), 1.
540 Joseph Thomas Moore. *Pride Against Prejudice: The Biography of Larry Doby*, (New York: Praeger Publishers, a division of Greenwood Press, 1988), 20.

It was indeed a noble feat to rise above the torment of segregation, and there are few more appropriate settings than sports to make such a profound statement. History has shown time and again that in the sporting arena, the world's most controversial issues can be settled over no exchange of words, just skills and statistics. In fact, during the same time that Robinson began to integrate professional baseball, Joe Louis, a black American boxer, was emerging as the greatest fighter of his time, shattering that sport's racial barriers. Prominent African-American sports figures were giving hope to blacks everywhere that a bright future existed beyond the degradation and humiliation of racial prejudice.

But conditions did not change overnight. Prejudice was still widespread, and the barriers to entry into professional baseball were still high when, just 11 weeks after Robinson's debut, Larry Doby became only the second black baseball player to compete in the major leagues and the first to play in the American League.[541]

Doby's story has largely been untold. Most Americans are not aware that he was named to the American League All Star game for six straight years and had a stellar batting record throughout his career.[542] He led the American League twice in home runs, and for five seasons he had more than 100 runs batted in.[543] He is also referred to as one of the greatest defensive centerfielders of the time. Doby had the top fielding average of all American Leaguers at that position in 1954 and set a major league record of 164 consecutive errorless games in 1954 and 1955 — a mark that stood for 17 years.[544] Of the 11 African-American baseball players who entered the major leagues in the 1940s, Larry was the only one still in the game in 1959, when he finally retired from the baseball majors.[545]

Doby survived the same adverse conditions that Robinson faced, and continued to endure that pain throughout his major league career. Yet, unlike the more gregarious and widely publicized Robinson, biographer Joseph Thomas Moore says Doby was a quiet pioneer.

---

[541] Ibid, 43.
[542] Ibid, 121.
[543] Dave Anderson. "Sports of the Times: A Serious Statesman Of the Game," (New York: New York *Times*, June 20, 2003), www.nytimes.com/2003/06/20/sports/baseball/20anderson.html, accessed April 29, 2010.
[544] Robert E. Botsch, "Larry Doby," *African-Americans and South Carolina: History, Politics, and Culture,* University of South Carolina at Aiken, 2006), www.usca.edu/aasc/doby.htm, accessed April 29, 2010.
[545] Moore, Ibid, 121.

Robinson was indeed *first,* and as such, he became a spokesperson for black America. Doby remained publicly silent. Moore describes Doby as a proud player, but he also illustrates how Doby's humble and subdued character kept him out of the limelight. During his career, Larry got little recognition for his achievements; it took decades before he was rightfully credited for his accomplishments in baseball. Adding to his burden, Doby came into the Majors with no professional experience and little more than a few days of preparation on how to handle the pressure and ridicule that would inevitably follow his arrival.

But Larry Doby was as much a civil rights pioneer as was Jackie Robinson. He faced the same obstacles with quiet dignity and unyielding optimism. He was not bitter playing in the shadow of Robinson. And he continued to persevere despite the fact that his contributions — to baseball and to society — would go unacknowledged for years.

From an early age, Doby learned a sense of pride and dignity that became the foundation of his character and a critical factor in his ability to withstand the indignities of racial prejudice throughout his life. Doby's father died when Larry was only 11; soon after, his mother left the family to search for work in Patterson, New Jersey, leaving Doby to live with his grandmother in Camden, South Carolina.[546]

Growing up in the Jim Crow South was not easy for a young black man. Larry faced segregation and ridicule in every aspect of his life. But his grandmother helped instill in him a sense of self-worth, pride and independence. He became the man of the house, helping her where he could — tending to deliveries, laundry and cleaning for local white families. He regularly attended church, and recalled, "Somehow I got the feeling that church helped black people to be themselves. I liked that feeling. I think my grandmother did, too."[547]

Camden was also home to a wealthy white community, immersed in horseracing for which the area was widely known. Larry's neighborhood, dubbed "Black Bottom," was the poorest section of the town.

After graduation from the eighth grade in Camden, Doby's mother encouraged him to join her in Patterson, New Jersey, where she felt there were more educational and economic opportunities for a promising young African-American male. In Patterson, he lived with a

---

[546] Botsch, Ibid.
[547] Moore, Ibid, 8-9.

family friend in an integrated neighborhood while his mother worked in domestic services. He saw her just once a week, on her day off.[548]

Doby never had much of a family life, but he was able to find solace in sports, both on the streets and in organized activities in school.[549] At Patterson's Eastside High, he played on four varsity teams. He was the only African-American on his high school football and baseball teams, and one of only two on the basketball team.[550] Larry would socialize with his white teammates, tolerating the racism that surrounded them. At the movies, he was forced to sit away from the team in the third balcony, watching by himself and then joining the others for sodas afterward.[551] At games, he would bear the brunt of racial insults from both fans and rival players.[552]

Yet coaches and teammates remember that he was never one to "take on the racists," as Doby's recreational basketball coach, Wendell Williams, put it. Williams, a black man, would urge radical racial militancy on his players and didn't quite understand, according to Moore, why Larry and the other players — including white players — would not take part. At that time, Doby and his teammates didn't share Williams' level of black self-awareness.[553] This feeling never relented. As Doby's family and friends recall, he wanted to focus his energy on the positive people and things in his life.[554] He preferred to be "just plain me."[555]

Being "plain me" to Doby meant letting his talents speak for themselves.[556] They did, too. In four years at Eastside, he won 11 varsity letters, and on the day he was awarded his final letter, he received a standing ovation from the entire student body. In addition to his

---

548 Botsch, Ibid.

549 Ibid.

550 Jacobson, Ibid, 31.

551 Ibid.

552 Moore, Ibid, 15.

553 Moore, Ibid, 15.

554 Harvey Araton, "Sports at the Times: Larry Doby Knew It Was About Home," The New York *Times*, June 24, 2003, www.nytimes.com/2003/06/24/ sports/sports-of-the-times-larry-doby-knew-it-was-about-home.html, accessed April 30, 2010.

555 Moore, Ibid, 17.

556 Justice B. Hill. "Doby stood tall in the face of adversity. While a pioneer, 'hero'may describe Doby best," The Official Web Site of the Cleveland Indians, June 19, 2003, cleveland.indians.mlb.com/news/article.jsp?ymd=20030619 &content_id= 383394&vkey=news_cle&fext=.jsp&c_id=cle, accessed April 30, 2010.

baseball skills, Doby was an exceptional running back on Eastside's football team. His outstanding play was instrumental in leading the team to the state championship. And when Eastside was denied an invitation to a postseason bowl game in Florida because Doby was black, neither the coach nor other members of the team considered kicking him off the team so they could play. The entire team stood unanimously behind Larry.[557]

Doby maintained a strong focus on sports, playing on several semi-pro and professional sports teams during the off seasons in high school. In 1938, he was selected to play with the Newark Eagles, the local Negro League baseball team. It had been against league rules for high school students to play, but Doby's raw talent drove Eagles' managers to sign him under the alias "Larry Walker from Los Angeles" and thus protect his amateur status.[558] Former Eagles' player Monte Irvin, who went on to play with the New York Giants and Chicago Cubs, watched Doby play at Eastside and remembers, "When I saw that swing, I knew all the stories about this kid did not exaggerate. He was going to be a star, somewhere, some day."[559] Doby signed a contract with the Eagles that year for $300. Headlines declared, "Signing of Larry Walker Rejuvenates Newark Eagles," and columns raved over his talent. During those first games of his professional baseball career, Doby batted .391 in the 26 games for which his records exist.[560]

Following high school graduation, Doby played with the Eagles in the 1942 season, now under his given name.[561] The Negro Leagues provided some of his happiest memories.[562] The players were among the best in American baseball history, and the camaraderie was exceptional. Players endured constant travel, less-than-ideal living conditions and little sleep. Few would have been able to tolerate the conditions if they had not loved the game, Jacob Margolies explains in *The Negro Leagues*. Players typically traveled in crowded cars; if a team was lucky enough to have a bus, the players often did the driving. Then, if they were lucky enough to find a restaurant willing to serve blacks, then the

---

[557] Moore, Ibid, 15.
[558] Ibid, 20.
[559] Lew Freedman, *African American Pioneers of Baseball: A Biographical Encyclopedia*, (Westport, Conn., Greenwood Press, 2007), 111.
[560] Moore, Ibid, 20.
[561] Botsch, Ibid.
[562] Moore, Ibid, 37.

players would not be forced to eat their meals on the bus, as was often the case. Barnstorming during the off-season brought in extra money, but players were forced to sleep in cars, buses or in some cases on the side of the road or in rail stations.[563]

Still, the Negro Leaguers played with heart, despite constant reminders of their bleak prospects of making it to the majors. Big league club presidents, team managers and sportswriters would describe it as unconscionable for blacks to join white players in the game. There was a belief, sometimes widespread, that black players were significantly more talented than white players; Negro League players would crave for match-ups against their white counterparts to prove it was true.[564]

Yet baseball's commissioners would have nothing of it. In the game's early years, Negro National League President Andrew "Rube" Foster attempted to organize match-ups between his and the major league teams. Baseball Commissioner Judge Kenesaw Mountain Landis detested the idea, reportedly replying, "Mr. Foster, when you beat our teams, it gives us a black eye." While Landis could not prevent his major leaguers from forming their own touring squads in the off-season, he would not allow them to wear their major league uniforms, guarding against the chance they would play a black team.[565]

The Negro Leagues were packed with talent, and Doby was one of the finest. Sportswriter Justice B. Hill has noted that players in the Negro Leagues knew how exceptional Doby was, and many thought either he or Monte Irvin would be the first to break baseball's color barrier. But according to Hill, Doby and the others understood the unlikelihood of ever playing for a major league team.

After a brief time at Long Island University, Doby was drafted into the Navy. Almost every one of the thousand recruits in his all-black camp were called to mess duty, but Doby was immediately noticed for his impeccable fitness and physical ability. Consequently, he was assigned as his camp's physical fitness instructor, spending whatever free time he had playing for his camp's sports teams and organizing recreational activities for the other servicemen.[566] His talents were further affirmed by one serviceman, Mickey Vernon, the renowned first

---

563 Jacob Margolies, *The Negro Leagues: The Story of Black Baseball*, (New York: Franklin Watts, 1993), 34 — 35.
564 Moore, Ibid, 35.
565 Margolies, Ibid, 28 — 29.
566 Robert E. Botsch, "Larry Doby."

baseman for the Washington Senators, who often discussed with Doby his immense potential as a player.[567]

Then in October 1945, Brooklyn Dodgers' General Manager Branch Rickey signed Jackie Robinson to a minor league contract with the Montreal Royals of the International League. Doby's life instantly changed. "My main thing was to become a teacher and coach somewhere in New Jersey, but when I heard about Jackie, I decided to concentrate on baseball," he said. "Everyone had said to me that I could."[568] It represented the opportunity of a lifetime and swept away any thoughts of returning to college.

Doby returned to New Jersey to play for the Newark Eagles again in 1946. The dugouts were filled with talk of Jackie Robinson's signing to Montreal. According to Doby biographer Moore, the news gave African-American players hope of advancing to the majors. At the same time, however, Doby and others found the news of Robinson's signing somewhat disconcerting; they believed there were Negro League players, especially Doby, who were far more talented. Nevertheless, Doby and his Eagles teammates did not let up. He batted .348 that season, and led the Eagles to the 1946 Negro World Series against the Kansas City Monarchs.[569] Newark won in seven games, the Eagles' first and only Negro League championship.[570] The league disbanded in 1948 as black players gained opportunities to play in the majors.

Doby returned to New Jersey for the 1947 season with the Eagles, batting .458 in the season's first half. While there was a great deal of chatter about Robinson in the National League, Bill Veeck, owner of the Cleveland Indians, was reportedly on the lookout for a promising African-American rookie; Doby's sizzling numbers had not gone unnoticed, and he emerged as a prime candidate. Speculation aside, however, there were no guarantees. Then, in the beginning of the 1947 season, Robinson made his debut with the Dodgers. Doby's introduction to the American League Indians came just weeks later.[571]

A number of factors worked against Doby's entry into the majors. Veeck had actively pursued baseball's integration for years. In 1942, he

---

[567] Moore, Ibid, 26.
[568] Ibid, 29.
[569] Ibid, 34.
[570] "Newark Eagles," Negro League Baseball Players Association Web Site, www.nlbpa.com/newark_eagles.html, accessed April 30, 2010.
[571] Moore, Ibid, 39 — 42.

attempted to purchase the bankrupt Philadelphia Phillies with intentions of introducing the first African-American players to baseball.[572] But according to Steve Jacobson, in *Carrying Jackie's Torch*, Veeck could not realistically have been the man to force the collapse of baseball's color barrier. He was from Cleveland. He wasn't as powerful as Rickey had been in Brooklyn. He didn't possess Rickey's profound Christian image.

Doby was also less prepared for the tests that awaited him than was Robinson, which has led some to conclude that his assimilation into major league baseball may have actually been more difficult.[573] Cal Fussman, in his book *After Jackie: Pride, Prejudice and Baseball's Forgotten Heroes*, described the careful managing of Robinson's introduction to the league by Rickey. Robinson also had experience traveling and interacting with other white players when he played with Montreal in the International League. From this, he gained maturity, a deeper understanding of the game and a stronger foundation upon which to build. Basically, Robinson had a support system that Doby didn't, thus giving him a significant edge in dealing with the intense insults and ridicule that accompanied a rising African-American star.[574]

A number of sportswriters and authors have also noted that the challenges Doby faced and overcame as a black ballplayer have been largely — and unfairly — ignored. In 1997, *Sports Illustrated* ran an editorial asking why Doby, still living, was being overlooked by historians.[575] He offered an answer: "You didn't hear much about what I was going through because the media didn't want to repeat the same story."[576] Translated, the blanket media coverage of Robinson's experience provided what Fussman said was "a different sort of protection" for the Dodger star.[577]

---

[572] Ibid, 22 — 23.

[573] Murray Chass, "Baseball; Doby Again Follows Robinson," New York *Times*, March 4, 1998, www.nytimes.com/1998/03/04/sports/baseball-doby-again-follows-robinson.html, accessed April 30, 1998.

[574] Cal Fussman, *After Jackie: Pride, Prejudice and Baseball's Forgotten Heroes: An Oral History*, (New York: ESPN Publishing, 2007), 79 — 80.

[575] New World Encyclopedia, "Larry Doby," www.newworldencyclopedia.org /entry/Larry_Doby, accessed May 3, 2010.

[576] Claire Smith, "Larry Doby, Who Broke a Color Barrier, Dies at 79," *New York Times*, June 19, 2003, www.nytimes.com/2003/06/20/sports/larry-doby-who-broke-a-color-barrier-dies-at-79.html, accessed May 3, 2010.

[577] Cal Fussman, *After Jackie: Pride, Prejudice and Baseball's Forgotten Heroes: An Oral History*, (New York: ESPN Publishing, 2007), 80.

Doby received no such preparation or protection. He was approached mid-season with the Newark Eagles in 1947 by Veeck and the Indians' scouts and told he was set to begin playing for the American League team immediately. The transition was anything but smooth, due in part, Moore says, to Veeck's rush to bring Doby up to the Indians.

Players received word that Doby would be joining the team just hours before his first game. Cleveland manager Lou Boudreau attempted to mitigate the potential hostility that would arise upon Doby's arrival, but his pregame efforts did little to ease tensions.[578] That evening, Doby entered an eerily quiet dugout. More than 25 players were in full uniform. Most faces were turned to the floor.[579] Four Indians denied a welcoming hand to the unfamiliar player. "Two of the four turned their backs on me," Larry remembers. "And nobody said, 'Congratulations.' "[580] Doby was told to suit up, and not another word was uttered as the team filed out of the locker room.[581] On the field, before that first game, he stood alone, rejected while the other players found teammates to warm up with. Finally, second baseman Joe Gordon offered to throw the ball with him.[582]

Larry also had a difficult time finding his place professionally with the Indians. Manager Lou Boudreau did not assign him to a regular position.[583] In the Negro Leagues Larry had been an excellent shortstop and second baseman, but on the Indians both jobs were held by exceptional veteran players.[584]

Franklin Lewis wrote that Doby confessed to feeling nervous when starting out with the Indians: "I feel — well, more than nervous. I feel almost like I was going into a new and strange world." Larry had difficulty fielding simple grounders[585] and struck out in his first at bat.[586] Feeling out of place in more ways than one, Doby played in only a few games in 1947, batting a dismal .156.[587]

---

[578] Moore, Ibid, 46 — 47.
[579] Franklin Lewis, *The Cleveland Indians,* (Kent, Ohio: The Kent State University Press, 2006), 247.
[580] Anderson, Ibid.
[581] Lewis, Ibid, 248.
[582] Anderson, Ibid.
[583] Moore, Ibid, 58.
[584] Ibid.
[585] Lewis, Ibid, 247.
[586] Jacobson, Ibid, 34.
[587] Ibid.

But the less-than-stellar first year with the Indians seemed to be no setback. He was ecstatic when told of his chances of making the team in 1948 as an outfielder. New to the position and in serious competition with seven other promising outfielders, Doby spent the off-season preparing for tryouts by reading books on how to play the outfield and staying busy playing professional basketball for the Paterson Crescents. Yet this excitement was accompanied by anxiety, uneasiness and uncertainty about where he fit in with the Indians. The question of what position he would play also affected other players, who were concerned about their own security on the team.[588]

Doby had to bear these feelings largely on his own. In the early days of his career, he had no black teammates with whom he could share his emotions. He spent the long weeks of spring training in segregated housing, as hotel owners felt his presence would "hurt business." During the regular season, his traveling escort, a black man assigned to lodge with him on away games, rarely spoke and provided little comfort. The two would simply eat dinner together after each game, then retreat to their rooms for the night. Doby recalls "not having another player to communicate with, talk over the game with after it's over and start me thinking about the next game."[589]

But Doby never complained — about this or any of the other indignities he faced. He would never speak out in opposition to racist umpires, fans or teammates. Instead, he kept his feelings to himself, dealing with his anger and frustrations in private. Interestingly, Larry found a confidant in Robinson. The two would talk through their frustrations — from sleeping in segregated hotel rooms to heckling from fans who would scream racial obscenities from the stands.[590] He was also careful not to take his pain home with him. His children describe him as one who never spoke of the "people who didn't treat him well"— only mentioning the "good guys."[591] He told stories of the Joe Gordons and Bill Veecks who were willing to risk the disapproval of some of the public and their peers for the sake of Doby, baseball and civil rights.[592]

This was how he dealt with prejudice throughout his life. He coped with his pain alone — unwilling to let the world see the hardships that

---

[588] Moore, Ibid, 67 — 68.
[589] Ibid, 68 — 69.
[590] Jacobson, Ibid, 32 — 33.
[591] Fussman, Ibid, 35.
[592] Jacobson, Ibid, 32 — 33.

came with rising to success in an intolerant world. One of Doby's teammates from Eastside High School described his presence on the field as "stoic," a quality that may have led to later criticism by fellow teammates and the media that his personality was too closed off. Yet he would be quick to respond by explaining how accustomed he had been to loneliness — given his ever-changing family life — and explained that this was simply his way of dealing with pain.[593] Still, it was a no-win situation. When defending his manner of coping with racism, Doby explained:

> People don't understand what it is. Who tells you about the balls you hit hard that weren't hits? Who tells you he should have had the ball you were charged with an error on? What do you do when everybody goes out of the ballpark after a game and you go alone? It's a loneliness where you're glad the next day comes, because you know you're back in the ballpark. The best time was the time on the field.[594]

Fortunately, Doby's playing was speaking for him. He impressed coaches with his phenomenal fielding and batting during spring training in 1948 and easily made the team. That year, the Cleveland Indians, ridiculed for 28 years, won the American League Pennant. Doby — who could run, throw and hit — played a key role. Then, in the World Series matchup against the Boston Braves, he led the Indians to their first World Series title.[595] During game four, he hit a home run off Johnny Sain to give the Indians a lead of three games to one for the series,[596] making Larry Doby the first black player to hit a home run in World Series history.[597] Afterward, Doby and winning pitcher Steve Gromek shared an embrace captured in a photograph that shocked the nation. The picture was one of the first to show affection between black and white athletes and is considered by Doby to be one of his most prized

---

593 Moore, Ibid, 16 — 17.
594 Jacobson, Ibid, 32 — 33.
595 Lewis, Ibid, 240 — 273.
596 Moore, Ibid, 82.
597 "Larry Doby," Wikipedia, en.wikipedia.org/wiki/Larry_Doby, accessed May 3, 2010.

possessions — as important as any accolade he ever received.[598] In his Hall of Fame speech, Doby said of the photograph, "America really needed that picture, and I'm proud I was able to give it to them."[599]

As the years rolled on, the sport began to wear on Doby's body. Stress, due less to physical strain and more to the years spent harvesting the pain from the indignities of discrimination, had given him terrible ulcers. His muscles easily became sore and cramped when he played. By the end of the 1955 season, he had become expendable to the Indians. He was traded several times until 1959, when he finally retired as a player with the White Sox. These trades, Moore explained, were hard on Doby because they rekindled memories of his insecure youth.[600]

Injured and out of baseball as a player, Larry was at a loss over what to do next. But he was determined to stay in the game somehow. Following his recovery from surgery to repair baseball-related injuries, he kept busy for several years in various roles that included scouting for several major league teams. Then in the summer of 1962, he joined fellow player and friend Don Newcombe to play for the Chunichi Dragons of Nagoya in the Japanese League. It was difficult for him and Newcombe to get back into shape, and neither started out well. But Larry found his hitting groove, and the Dragons moved from last place to second place by season's end. He and Newcombe also offered batting, fielding and pitching lessons to their teammates. Their role in integrating the Japanese League was noted by President John F. Kennedy as a positive step in U.S. efforts to strengthen relations with Japan, and Japanese baseball writer Kiyoshi Nakagawa says they ignited a "foreigner boom" in Japanese baseball.[601]

Following the season with Chunichi, Doby kept busy opening and operating a liquor store in Patterson. But he wanted back into baseball. Thus began phase 2 of his professional career — the pursuit of a career managing a major league team. In the spring of 1969, he took his first coaching position with the Montreal Expos' farm team. He was respected for his baseball intelligence and remembered as an especially exceptional batting instructor who could watch a batter's swing and easily identify hitting problems. He was quickly promoted to full-time

---

[598] Moore, Ibid, 3 — 4.
[599] Fussman, Ibid, 34.
[600] Moore, Ibid, 117 — 121.
[601] Moore, Ibid, 123 — 125.

batting coach for the Expos. At this juncture in his career, Doby felt baseball had reached the point where color was irrelevant.[602]

His dream to manage a major league team became more focused. Yet, much to his dismay, it did not take long for him to see that his hopes would be impeded by the same discrimination that was so rampant in the earlier years of his career. As soon as he made strides, white managers would place him at the bottom of the coaching totem pole, often assigning him to positions for their clubs' lesser farm teams. There was criticism from team presidents and players that black men simply didn't have what it took to manage a professional baseball team.[603]

Regardless of the anger or betrayal he may have felt, Doby once again decided to let his performance make the case for his potential as a manager. He accepted an offer to manage Zulia of Maracaibo, Venezuela, in the winter of 1971 – 72, leading the team to a first-place finish. He then returned to coach with Montreal and later accepted a coaching position with the Indians where there might be managing opportunities later on. Just before the 1975 season with Cleveland, word spread of an open managing position. Larry was rumored to have been a top choice and had high hopes of being selected. But when the decision had been made, no one had the decency to tell him he had been passed up for Indians' outfielder Frank Robinson, who thus became the first African-American to manage a major league baseball team. Indians owners' said Doby lacked sufficient experience as a manager, ignoring the fact that he had successfully led the club's farm team and was said to have better rapport with the Indians players than Robinson did. Doby's response to Robinson's appointment—and to his own subsequent release—was to simply wish the new skipper well and say that he "could not waste any time or energy to even think about being bitter."[604]

After returning to the Expos as a coach, Doby finally got what he wanted: In the middle of the 1978 season, Veeck named him manager of the Chicago White Sox. But the dream was short-lived. Saddled with a team that possessed just one .300 hitter and one outstanding defensive player — centerfielder Chuck Lemon in both cases — victories were hard to come by. And when ticket sales hadn't improved after Doby's

---

[602] Ibid, 131 – 132.
[603] Ibid, 135 – 138.
[604] Moore, Ibid, 133 – 142.

appointment, it was reported that Veeck used this to justify letting him go at the end of the season.[605]

Doby remained in sports for several years, coaching for various baseball teams and taking on front-office positions in basketball and then later in baseball.[606] It wasn't until the 1990s that baseball woke up to the fact that he was every bit as deserving of recognition as Jackie Robinson. In 1994 the Cleveland Indians retired the No. 14 jersey Doby had worn in his 10 seasons playing there. That same year he was selected to the South Carolina Athletic Hall of Fame. In 1997 the Cleveland Indians hosted a week of tributes to Doby, culminating with Cleveland Mayor Michael R. White's announcement that five playgrounds were to be named Larry Doby All-Star Playgrounds.[607] He was finally given the ultimate acclaim in 1998 with his induction into the Hall of Fame in Cooperstown.[608]

Doby did not resent the overdue honors, just as he had no bitterness toward Jackie Robinson or Frank Robinson or even the racists across America who had taunted him during his playing days. Rather, he focused on what he considered to be his real triumphs.[609] When he shared his history with students in Northfield, Minnesota, during a Carleton College program founded by former baseball commissioner Fay Vincent, Doby said:

> It was a learning lesson for baseball and the country. If we all look back, we can see that baseball helped make this a better country for us all, a more comfortable country for us all, especially for those of us who have grands and great-grands. Kids are our future and we hope baseball has given them some idea

[605] Ibid, 148 – 164.

[606] Fay Vincent, "Larry Doby Played With Dignity and Without Bitterness," *New York Times*, June 22, 2003, www.nytimes.com/2003/06/22/ sports/ baseball/ 22VINC.html, accessed May 3, 2010.

[607] New World Encyclopedia, "Larry Doby," www.newworldencyclopedia.org/ entry/Larry_Doby, accessed May 12, 2010.

[608] Vincent, Ibid.

[609] Claire Smith, "Larry Doby, Who Broke a Color Barrier, Dies at 79," *New York Times*, June 20, 2003, www.nytimes.com/2003/06/20/sports/larry-doby-who-broke-a-color-barrier-dies-at-79.html.

of what it is to live together and how we can get along, whether you be black or white.'[610]

Joseph Thomas Moore concluded that Doby, who died in 2003 from cancer, did an amazing thing for baseball by showing aspiring African-American baseball players — and all Americans, for that matter — that it is not necessary to be an immortal like Jackie Robinson to be successful. With this lesson, underscored by his optimism and quiet dignity, Larry Doby gave common men hope and proved that life's bitter trials can truly be blessings in disguise.

Doby's determined optimism and legacy continue to inspire kids all over America and most especially the citizens of his small Southern home town of Camden, South Carolina, where many young men have been inspired to follow in his footsteps into professional athletics.

---

[610] New World Encyclopedia, "Larry Doby," www.newworldencyclopedia.org/entry/Larry_Doby, accessed May 12, 2010.

# EPILOGUE

In addition to these historic figures, most who have long since left this earth, America has begun to see the rebirth of a new generation of optimism and bold leaders. I have had the good fortune of knowing one of these visionaries — strong, determined and unwaveringly optimistic.

In a 1943 letter to U.S. Cavalry Brigadier General H.D. Chamberlin, General George S. Patton wrote that wars were won not by the "apparent virtue" of defense, but by "continued optimism and a fighting spirit." This is a lesson that is not lost on one of today's heroes—Dan DiMicco.

While DiMicco may not be a household name to most, as chairman president, and CEO of Nucor Steel, he is one of the nation's most respected business leaders. No less than Jim Cramer, the sometimes bombastic host of cable television's *Mad Money*, has said, "The steel industry is not known for its visionaries since (Andrew) Carnegie. But Dan's the closest to one you are going to find among present-day management."[611] Indeed, DiMicco has been widely praised for his ability to not only sustain Nucor's leadership as the world's top steel producer but also as the industry's top sustainable company. And he has done it with a blend of toughness, strategic understanding, intuition and an active, no-holds-barred optimism that would have made Patton proud.

DiMicco would likely agree that his success, in many ways, is rooted in Nucor, its culture and a dream: the dream of using recycled scrap steel to cast flat-rolled sheet metal from a once developing technology called the electric-arc-fired furnace.

In September 2000, Nucor named DiMicco CEO. DiMicco and his team turned Nucor into the nation's largest steelmaker. The growth under his leadership has been striking: By 2008, the company had more than doubled in size, due largely through 22 acquisitions. When he took over in 2000, Nucor made $311 million on $4.59 billion in sales. By 2008, those numbers had risen substantially, as the company made $1.47 billion on $16.6 billion in sales. In 2006, *Business Week* named him the country's "Most Inspiring Boss." Cramer, in a nationally

---

[611] John Downey, *Charlotte Business Journal*, "Forging Nucor's Path to the Top." January 2, 2009. Copyright 2009, American City Business Journals Inc., charlotte.bizjournals.com/charlotte/stories/2009/01/05/story2.html , accessed March 12, 2009.

televised interview, crowned him "The King of Steel." *The Charlotte Business Journal* honored him as Business Person of the Year in 2008.

Characteristically, DiMicco credits his management team for that success — a quality that he also shares with Patton, who freely recognized both team and individual performance. After the U.S. general's triumph at Bastogne, a small town in Belgium whose strategic value lay in its position as a hub for several major highways, Robert S. Allen, a syndicated newspaper columnist who served on Patton's staff during the war, wrote, "It was all wrought quietly and efficiently by a teamwork without parallel in the ETO (European Theater of Operations), a teamwork rooted deeply in great know-how, in great confidence in itself and its Commander, and in great fighting spirit."[612]

The comparison with Patton can be seen more than 60 years later, in DiMicco's words in Nucor's 2009 mid-year report: "Our team is already capitalizing on Nucor's position of strength — a position of strength arising from our balance sheet, low cost and highly flexible production capabilities, unrivaled product diversification, and—most importantly — Nucor's extremely productive and innovative work force."[613] And when *The Harvard Business Review* named DiMicco and the Nucor management among the "Best Performing CEOs in the World" in January 2010, he said, "This ranking is an honor for every member of the Nucor team. The 21,000 men and women of Nucor are working safely, working hard and working together to reward our shareholders with attractive long-term returns on their valuable capital. The dedication and talents of my teammates are why I am very confident that Nucor's best years are still ahead of us."

At 58 years old, a relatively young age for a senior executive, Dan DiMicco has already become an icon and a living legend in the U.S. steel industry. And while he thoroughly understands, supports and perpetuates Nucor's traditions and culture, it took a series of career twists and turns for his professional journey to intersect with the steelmaker — a journey that was not without a few surprise stops along the way. Appropriately, it was a journey that first found direction in optimism.

---

[612] Farago, 710.
[613] PR Newswire, iStockAnalyst, "Nucor Announces Guidance For Its Second Quarter Results," June 16, 2009,
www.istockanalyst.com/article/viewiStockNews/articleid/3301881#, accessed December 10, 2009.

As a high school student in Mount Kisco, New York, in the mid-1960s, DiMicco was swept up in President John F. Kennedy's optimistic vow to put a man on the moon by decade's end. "Engineering became a big thing," he recalled. "I had an aptitude in math. So I went through high school in math and science courses and had the idea that I would work at NASA some day."[614] He went to Brown University but "electrical engineering and myself did not take."[615] Still hoping to join NASA or somehow get involved with the space program, he turned his academic interests toward materials science and metallurgical engineering.

Smart enough to know that he needed additional education to get the job he wanted, DiMicco considered his options. He had applied to engineering schools as well as business schools after getting out of Brown and had been accepted by both. But the experience eventually boiled down to neither career nor educational opportunities. It boiled down to family.

"You know, my mother and father worked very hard throughout their entire life," he told the *Charlotte Business Journal*. "My mom worked. Part of the reason I got to go to college was she was working. I worked in college cleaning bathrooms and other things to make some spending money and what have you. I had a few scholarships that helped. So being able to pay your own way was very important. I was the oldest child in a family of five.

"So when I got the acceptance letters from the business schools and the engineering schools, I looked at 'em and the business schools were very happy to loan me $5,000 a year to go there and the engineering schools were very happy to give me free tuition and a stipend of $330 a month. I said, 'Decision made.'"[616]

With a master of science in metallurgy and materials science from Penn, he took a job in a research capacity with Republic Steel in Cleveland in 1975. It was not long, however, before he and one of his engineering co-workers began hearing about Nucor. They were especially intrigued by its workplace culture, which even today is considered unique — and positively so — in the business world. "(W)e started reading about this company that was called Nucor — its culture, its pay-for-performance system," DiMicco said. "You got ahead by doing

[614] Downey, Ibid, 1.
[615] Ibid.
[616] Downey, Ibid, 2.

a good job. And if you did not do a good job, you did not get ahead. We said 'Aw, that's the kind of company we want to work for.'"[617]

To DiMicco, who—like Patton—was dedicated, focused, and unafraid of work or a challenge — Nucor must have seemed like a dream opportunity. But for a variety of reasons, he elected not to pursue it. Then one day his friend, who had gone to business school, called and announced he had taken a position at a Nucor startup in Plymouth, Utah. There was a metallurgical job opening at the facility. Would DiMicco be interested?

The decision was not difficult. DiMicco had served as research metallurgist and project leader for seven years at Republic. But the 1980-81 recession was gripping northern Ohio, and he was working two jobs after a series of pay cuts and struggling to make ends meet. So he packed up the family belongings, the dog, one small child and one very pregnant wife and took a chance on the opportunity in Utah. In November 1982, Dan DiMicco had found a home as plant metallurgist and manager of quality control for Nucor Steel. Six years later, he became melting and casting manager.

In the years that followed, DiMicco attracted opportunity like a magnet attracts steel. He accepted an offer from management to oversee a new plant being built in Blytheville, Arkansas, the result of a joint venture between Nucor and Japanese steelmaker Yamato steel. As general manager, he motivated and inspired his team to significantly improve productivity, and the plant grew to more than double its original size.

DiMicco's similarities to the colorful American General Patton are striking. He has kept Nucor's corporate team small and nimble — there are just 75 administrative employees in Charlotte — and pushes responsibilities to managers in the field, both of which provide the kind of speed and mobility in business that Patton so valued in combat. Patton also saw the importance of trying new tactics and weapons, particularly as technology advanced. Similarly, DiMicco has been consistently committed to expansion and improvements at the plant level that have included new technologies and processes designed not only to improve productivity but also to raise the industry bar for environmental responsibility.

---

[617] Downey, Ibid.

Those strategies have paid off. Nucor announced that for the full year 2008, consolidated net earnings totaled $1.83 billion. At a time when most companies' performance fell well below expectations, Nucor's consolidated net sales for 2008 increased 43 percent to a record $23.7 billion. And while the company was not exempt from effects of the 2009 global recession — steel prices dropped 50 percent and plants operated at half capacity — DiMicco was able to continue a storied corporate tradition: No one was laid off. This was an important and core objective for DiMicco. He maintains without equivocation, while other short-sighted CEOs look at short-term profits, that "What is good for America is good for Nucor."

Then there is the matter of personality. Patton was famous for saying exactly what he was thinking, the consequences notwithstanding. DiMicco is just as likely to speak his mind and is equally unafraid to stick to his guns. Writer Rebecca Rolfes put it like this:

> He is described by his peers in the metals industry as "an old style steel guy." DiMicco, a metallurgist by training, pounds the table at speaking engagements and town hall meetings from the House Ways and Means Committee to Bourbonnais, Illinois.
>
> His cause: American manufacturing and how unfair trade practices are eroding good paying jobs for American workers and, hence, the fabric of national society.
>
> DiMicco does not tiptoe around any of the related issues. He understands but does not care about the complexities and niceties of multi-lateral trade negotiations. He does not mind stepping on the toes of industry advocates trying to navigate Capitol Hill or win membership dues. He told an audience at the Southern Growth Policies Board conference in June 2005 that the United States' position on trade needs "to be precisely the opposite of their approach" and that "our trade laws need to be more easily accessible

to small as well as large companies."[618]

Also like Patton, DiMicco is not one to shrink from a challenge. In the Bastogne operation, Patton was faced with what some saw as an impossible task. Major Charles Codman, one of the general's staff members, noted the challenge:

> It was a seemingly impossible undertaking to which Patton was now committing himself. As Codman put it "To disengage three divisions actually in combat and launch them over more than a hundred miles of icy roads straight into the heart of a major attack of unprecedented violence presented problems which few commanders would have undertaken to resolve in that length of time."[619]

And yet, Patton threw himself into the task with confidence, enthusiasm and optimism, refusing to withdraw or regroup, guided by his favorite quote, from Georges Danton, a leading figure in the French Revolution: "Audacity, audacity, always audacity."

That same kind of audacity — emboldened but not tempered by optimism — has driven DiMicco in good, difficult, challenging and opportunistic times. When he assumed the company's leadership in 2000, there were questions as to whether Nucor's "nimble, entrepreneurial culture could survive the imperative to make it larger."[620] The steel industry had still not rebounded, and most CEOs would likely have a more cautious path, moving slowly and waiting for the economic storms to pass. DiMicco, on the other hand, took Nucor in a very different direction: growth through acquisition. He was boldly optimistic, believing that times would get better and pursing a strategy to ensure Nucor was in a position to seize any potential business

---

[618] Rebecca Rolfes, "The Working Man's Evangelist," *Forward Online*, A Global Perspective of Metals Service Center Institute, January/February 2006 issue, forward.msci.org/articles/0206working.cfm#, accessed March 30, 2010.
[619] Farago, 708.
[620] Downey, Ibid, 1.

opportunity. In essence, he put a piece of Patton's wisdom into action: "Take calculated risks. That is quite different from being rash."[621]

DiMicco's strategy was being implemented during a period in which the industry was undergoing major restructuring. Weak companies went out of business. The stronger ones joined forces to become even bigger and stronger. Under DiMicco's aggressive leadership, Nucor spent more than $1 billion, buying 10 steel mills at bargain basement prices. Many of these plants were located in the Deep South where Nucor's timely acquisitions revived struggling businesses, saved jobs and created new ones. But it was not expansion for its own sake, nor growth based solely on balance sheet considerations. In making key decisions, DiMicco had the audacity to look at jobs created, the stimulus to other business in the community and the positive potential effect of Nucor's involvement in critical local issues such as education. That kind of thinking has made Nucor facilities among the largest employers in their host communities and have earned the local mills a much-deserved reputation for "giving back" to the cities and towns they call home.

DiMicco's steady rise to the top of Nucor, as well as his success upon arrival, is no doubt a function of his competitive nature. He had four siblings and was a rugged performer on his high school and college football teams, and he went up against some of the country's brightest students to earn two Ivy League degrees — a blue-collar kid who made it by hard work and pure initiative. His competitive nature also instilled in DiMicco a strong sense of fair play.

It is important, even essential, to note that DiMicco's frankness is fueled by an undying belief in America. He doesn't try to hide it, either. During testimony before the Congressional Steel Caucus, he discussed the value of Buy American laws, which he said "are consistent with our international obligations." As he continued, DiMicco's passion, and his patriotism, grew even stronger.

DiMicco's patriotism — reflected in Nucor's culture — has even been recognized by the U.S. Department of Defense for unwavering support of American troops. In 2007, the Department announced that Nucor was one of just 16 U.S. corporations awarded the year's "Secretary

---

[621] Dorie McCullough Lawson, "Letter of Gen. George S. Patton Jr. to his son, George S. Patton III on D-Day, June 6, 1944," *Posterity: Letters of Great Americans to Their Children*, (New York: Broadway Books, an imprint of the Doubleday Broadway Publishing Group, a division of Random House, 2004), 100.

of Defense Employer Support Freedom Award." The honor is given to a special group of employers for having provided exceptional support to their employees who are also men and women voluntarily serving in our National Guard and Reserve.[622]

None of this is especially surprising. Dan DiMicco is both a product of and a poster child for America. He is proof that hard work and dedication have their rewards. He has never lost compassion for working men and women, either in his plants or in America. He intensely dislikes rule-breakers. He sticks up for people and is unafraid to go nose-to-nose with anyone who pursues an agenda he believes is unfair or unjust. He speaks in a voice of optimism that resonates with blue-collar honesty.

Gen. George S. Patton Jr. once famously said, "It is better to fight for something than live for nothing." He could have been talking about Dan DiMicco. Because no matter what the fight — an economic downturn, unfair trade practices, competitive challenges, safety in the workplace — Dan DiMicco fights. And that's important — not just for Nucor, the steel industry and U.S. manufacturing, but for America as well.

Dan's life is an example of undaunted optimism, hard work and determination by a blue collar New York kid who never forgot who he was or how he got where he did. Dan is my friend and an inspiration. I know that his actions are, to paraphrase the late Bobby Kennedy, "creating a ripple of hope that ... can overcome even the greatest barriers."[623]

---

[622] Department of Defense Press Release, "Department of Defense Announces 2007 Secretary of Defense Employer Support Freedom Award Recipients," July 20, 2007, www.esgr.org/news.asp , accessed December 11, 2009.
[623] Robert F. Kennedy, "Day of Affirmation Address," University of Capetown, Capetown, South Africa, June 6, 1966,
www.jfklibrary.org/Historical+Resources/Archives/Reference+Desk/Speeches/ RFK/Day+of+Affirmation+Address+News+Release.htm, accessed May 26, 2010. Entire quote: "Each time a man stands up for an ideal, or acts to improve the lot of others, or strikes out against injustice, he sends forth a tiny ripple of hope, and crossing each other from a million different centers of energy and daring, those ripples build a current which can sweep down the mightiest walls of oppression and resistance."

# THROUGH THE FIRE

Songwriter: Gerald Crabb

So many times I've questioned certain circumstances
Things I could not understand
Many times in trials, weakness blurs my vision
Then my frustration gets so out of hand
It's then I am reminded I've never been forsaken
I've never had to stand the test alone
As I look at all the victories the spirit rises up in me
And it's through the fire my weakness is made strong

He never promised that the cross would not get heavy
And the hill would not be hard to climb
He never offered our victories without fighting
But he said help would always come in time
Just remember when you're standing in the valley of decision
And the adversary says give in
Just hold on, our Lord will show up
And he will take you through the fire again

I know within myself that I would surely perish
But if I trust the hand of God, He'll shield the flames again

# THOMAS STOWE MULLIKIN

A committed environmental attorney, author, lecturer and soldier, Tom Mullikin leads the Government, Policy and Regulatory Affairs Team for Moore & Van Allen law firm. With a career spanning three decades working in campaigns and representing interests before local, state and federal government, Tom is passionate about igniting awareness and inspiring public participation in complex energy, environmental and health care concerns. His issue awareness and resolution models are nationally-acclaimed.

Tom is also the author of *The Maxims of Politics: Making Government Work*, *Sportsman Environmentalist*, *Global Solutions: Demanding Total Accountability for Climate Change*, and *Truck Stop Politics: Understanding the Emerging Force of Working Class America*. He is executive producer of The Whole Truth, an award-winning documentary on global climate change.

www.mullikinsmaxims.com